Diving & Snorkeling
Maldives

Casey Mahaney & Astrid Witte Mahaney

LONELY PLANET PUBLICATIONS
Melbourne • Oakland • London • Paris

Diving & Snorkeling Maldives
- A Lonely Planet Pisces Book

1st Edition – November 2001

Published by
Lonely Planet Publications Pty Ltd, ABN 36 005 607 983
90 Maribyrnong St., Footscray, Victoria 3011, Australia

Other offices
150 Linden Street, Oakland, California 94607, USA
10a Spring Place, London NW5 3BH, UK
1 rue du Dahomey, 75011 Paris, France

Photographs
by Casey Mahaney & Astrid Witte Mahaney
     (unless otherwise noted)

Front cover photograph
Diver admires soft corals and sweetlips at
     Okobe Thila, North Male' Atoll

Back cover photographs
Portrait of a friendly Napoleonfish
A coral-wreathed window at Kudaboli Thila,
     Felidhoo Atoll
Traditional Maldivian dhoni, by Michael Aw

Most of the images in this guide are available for
     licensing from **Lonely Planet Images**
     email: lpi@lonelyplanet.com.au

ISBN 1 86450 363 7

text & maps © Lonely Planet Publications Pty Ltd 2001
photographs © photographers as indicated 2001
dive site maps are Transverse Mercator projection

Printed by H&Y Printing Ltd., Hong Kong

Contents

Diving in the Maldives 34

North Male' Atoll (Kaafu) Dive Sites 41

South Male' Atoll (Kaafu) Dive Sites 58

Felidhoo Atoll (Vaavu) Dive Sites 68

Mulaku Atoll (Meemu) Dive Sites   80

Addu Atoll (Seenu) Dive Sites   85

South & North Nilandhoo Atolls (Dhaalu & Faafu) Dive Sites   88

Ari Atoll (Alifu) Dive Sites   95

South & North Maalhosmadulu Atolls (Baa & Raa) Dive Sites 113

Faadhippolhu Atoll (Lhaviyani) Dive Sites 119

Marine Life 125

Diving Conservation & Awareness 131

Listings 135

Index 149

Authors

Casey Mahaney & Astrid Witte Mahaney

Casey Mahaney and Astrid Witte Mahaney are internationally published photojournalists who specialize in underwater photography. They are the authors of five marine life identification guides and numerous scuba travel and destination guides. Every year they spend several months diving and taking photographs at destinations such as the Maldives. Having introduced thousands of divers to the magic of Pacific reefs, they now specialize in escorted live-aboard dive tours to exotic destinations worldwide. Find them on the internet at www.bluekirio.com.

From the Authors

We want to thank the people and organizations whose support and contributions of knowledge, expertise and dive vessels helped make this guide as complete and accurate as possible. Special thanks to Mike Spielmann, Werner Lau, Mary Eichler and Steve Ströbel, Abdul Haleem Thowfeeq, Norbert Probst, Giorgio Rosi Belliere, Keith Antell, Jürgen Schmiederer and Sascha Hamersky.

Photography Notes

Underwater, Casey and Astrid use a variety of cameras and formats. For macro and close-up photography they use the Nikon 8008s and N90s fitted with either a 60 or 105mm lens in an Ikelite or Nexus housing. For wide-angle shots they prefer the N90 with 18 and 20mm lenses in a Nexus housing. They use Ikelite 50 strobes mounted on Light & Motion pop-arms for macro work and Ikelite 200 strobes mounted on Ultralite arms for wide-angle shots. Topside, they work with their Nikon cameras and a variety of lenses, including zoom lenses. They prefer Fujichrome slide films such as Velvia and Provia for their brilliant color saturation.

Contributing Photographers

Casey Mahaney and Astrid Witte Mahaney took most of the photographs in this book. Thanks also to Michael Aw, Edward Snijders, James Lyon, Staeven Vallak, Norbert Probst, Dennis Wisken, John Borthwick and Gavin Anderson.

From the Publisher

This first edition was published in Lonely Planet's U.S. office under the guidance of Roslyn Bullas, the Pisces Books publishing manager. David Lauterborn edited the text and photos with buddy checks from Sarah Hubbard and Pelin Thornhill. Emily Douglas designed the cover and the book's interior. Navigating the nautical charts was cartographer Rachel Driver, who created the maps, with assistance from Sara Nelson and Brad Lodge. U.S. cartography manager Alex Guilbert supervised map production. Lindsay Brown reviewed the Marine Life section for scientific accuracy. Portions of the text were adapted from Lonely Planet's *Maldives.*

Pisces Pre-Dive Safety Guidelines

Before embarking on a scuba diving, skin diving or snorkeling trip, carefully consider the following to help ensure a safe and enjoyable experience:

- Possess a current diving certification card from a recognized scuba diving instructional agency (if scuba diving)
- Be sure you are healthy and feel comfortable diving
- Obtain reliable information about physical and environmental conditions at the dive site (e.g., from a reputable local dive operation)
- Be aware of local laws, regulations and etiquette about marine life and environment
- Dive at sites within your experience level; if possible, engage the services of a competent, professionally trained dive instructor or divemaster

Underwater conditions vary significantly from one region, or even site, to another. Seasonal changes can significantly alter site and dive conditions. These differences influence the way divers dress for a dive and what diving techniques they use.

There are special requirements for diving in any area, regardless of location. Before your dive, ask about environmental characteristics that can affect your diving and how trained local divers deal with these considerations.

Warning & Request

Things change—dive site conditions, regulations, topside information. Nothing stays the same for long. Your feedback on this book will be used to help update and improve the next edition. Excerpts from your correspondence may appear in *Planet Talk*, our quarterly newsletter, or *Comet*, our monthly email newsletter. Please let us know if you do not want your letter published or your name acknowledged.

Correspondence can be addressed to:
Lonely Planet Publications
Pisces Books
150 Linden Street
Oakland, CA 94607
email: pisces@lonelyplanet.com

Introduction

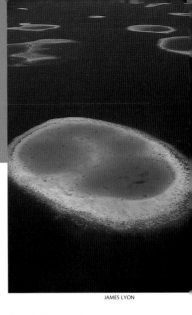

The Maldives draws visitors from all corners of the world. Many are mesmerized by the amazing brilliance of colors—lush green palm fronds, emerald lagoons and perfectly white beaches, all surrounded by a deep blue sea. Others are intrigued by the unique and colorful culture reflected in the faces of the Maldivian people, their fascinating mosques, exotic markets and unusual architecture.

JAMES LYON

Yet for divers it's the underwater wonders that set the Maldives above many other travel destinations. The same maze of shallow reefs that have proven so treacherous to seafarers over the centuries now delight divers and snorkelers with a wealth of marine life and stunning grotto formations. While hard corals took a hit from coral bleaching in 1998, the reefs remain cloaked in vibrant soft corals and sponges, and the fish life is astounding.

Although there are now nearly 90 resorts and more than 90 safari dive boats (live-aboards) in the Maldives, the archipelago can hardly be considered a victim of mass tourism. Careful planning has fostered an environmentally friendly tourist

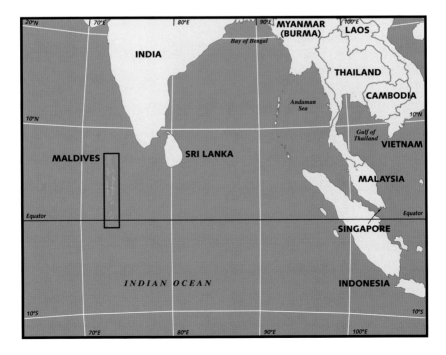

industry. Largely free of traffic, crime and crude commercialism, the country provides all the necessary creature comforts and then some. Of course, this quality of service comes at a cost. The Maldives is generally not considered a destination for low-budget backpackers, though you will find a few lower-priced guesthouses on the capital island, Male'.

To protect the sensitive Muslim culture, visitors to the Maldives are not allowed to simply drop in on any island they please. Tourists are restricted to the atolls that have been opened to tourism. This book covers dive sites in those tourist regions, including **North Male' Atoll** and **South Male' Atoll (Kaafu)**, **Felidhoo Atoll (Vaavu)**, **Mulaku Atoll (Meemu)**, **Addu Atoll (Seenu)**, **South & North Nilandhoo Atolls (Dhaalu & Faafu)**, **Ari Atoll (Alifu)**, **South & North Maalhosmadulu Atolls (Baa & Raa)** and **Faadhippolhu Atoll (Lhaviyani)**.

You'll find specific information on 78 of the Maldives' best dive sites, including location, depth, access and recommended diving expertise. You'll also learn about each site's underwater terrain and the marine life you may encounter. The Marine Life section presents photos of the Maldives' most common vertebrates and invertebrates, while the Overview section delivers information about the culture, geology and history of the Maldives. While this book is not intended to be a stand-alone travel guide, the Practicalities and Listings sections will help you prepare for a comfortable and enjoyable trip.

Most visitors enjoy their first close look at the Maldives over the graceful prow of a dhoni.

Overview

STAEVEN VALLAK

The 26 atolls comprising the Republic of the Maldives are grouped into 19 administrative districts. The letters of the Maldivian language (Dhivehi) are used to name these administrative atolls. Of the country's approximately 1,190 coral islands, only 202 are locally inhabited. The rest are officially referred to as uninhabited, although nearly 90 such islands serve as tourist resorts and many more are used for factories, airfields or agriculture.

According to 2000 estimates, the population is more than 300,000, with about 65,000 living in Male', the capital. Life in the fishing villages is almost entirely unaffected by contact with the outside world. Architecturally, these villages are unique. Most houses are made from coral rocks joined by mortar. Traditional Maldivian villages are also noted for their neat and orderly layout and for their cleanliness. On atolls open to tourism, some villages have set up souvenir shops, yet many of the traditional values remain.

All Maldivians are Muslims of the Sunni sect, a more liberal form of Islam than that practiced in some Arab countries. Prayers are held five times a day, at which time all shops and offices close for 15 minutes. No other religions or sects are present or permitted in the country.

The Maldives' economy is heavily based on fishing and tourism, as well as shipping. Agriculture accounts for less than 8% of the GDP, and nearly all food items are imported.

Reports of Our Death Are Greatly Exaggerated

In the wake of widespread coral bleaching during the El Niño in 1998, the media went wild with reports that 90% of all coral reefs in the Maldives were dead. Rumors quickly spread among divers that the islands were simply not worth a visit anymore. While it's true that the majority of shallow hard-coral gardens were severely hit by the bleaching (see "Coral Bleaching," page 131), most of the dive sites remain beautiful, studded with perfectly intact soft corals, colorful sponges and anemones. All underwater images in this book were taken in the wake of El Niño damage.

11

Geography

The Maldives archipelago stretches north-south some 800km (500 miles) across the Indian Ocean, 600km (370 miles) southwest of Sri Lanka. With a total land area of 298 sq km (116 sq miles), the islands are grouped into atolls that straddle the equatorial belt, the majority of islands lying just north of the equator. None of the islands is longer than 8km (5 miles) or higher than 3m (10ft) above sea level, ensuring perfect beaches but a notable absence of mountains and rivers.

Geology

Consisting of coral stone, rubble and sand, the Maldives islands sit atop an ancient submerged mountain range. Volcanic in origin, the mountains erupted from the seafloor some 65 million years ago. The resulting islands were simply the exposed peaks of these submarine volcanoes. Corals soon colonized the shorelines, creating fringing reefs. As the volcanoes became extinct, they subsided, while the reefs continued to grow upward. This development formed barrier reefs that enclosed the sinking islands within lagoons. Eventually the islands submerged completely, leaving only coral atolls encircling shallow lagoons.

Over time, sand and coral rubble accumulated atop the shallowest sections of the atolls, enabling plants to take root, although many of the islands remain largely barren, supporting only a limited range of plant life. Within the lagoons are scattered submerged coral pinnacles, as well as small islands formed by corals that built up until they broke the surface. Underwater, the pinnacles, channels and outer reef slopes are often carved with protruding terraces and caverns.

Officially, it's the vegetation that differentiates a Maldivian island from just a sandbank. The Dhivehi language includes a variety of words for island, such as *fushi*, which describes a large island with lots of plant life, and *finolhu*, describing a small island with very little vegetation. The word atoll itself derives from the Dhivehi word *atolu*.

DENNIS WISKEN

Maldivians use a variety of terms to describe their islands, each defined by its vegetation.

Are the Maldives Drowning?

While scientists blame El Niño for coral bleaching that swept the Maldives' reefs in the summer of 1998, the archipelago faces a far more serious threat from global warming. In this nation of sandbars and islands that top out less than 3m (10ft) above the surface, rising sea levels could submerge the atolls beneath the waves, à la Atlantis. Some studies predict that by 2100 sea levels could rise anywhere from 50cm (20 inches) to 1m (3ft), making such a dire scenario tragically credible.

In fear of becoming environmental refugees, Maldivians are preparing for the worst. With aid from Japan, the country has constructed a concrete seawall around much of Male', while breakwaters ring other islands. Since the coral reefs act as a natural protective barrier, the government has banned the use of coral as a building material. Meanwhile, schoolteachers and the nation's only TV channel continue to educate Maldivians about the potential consequences of global warming.

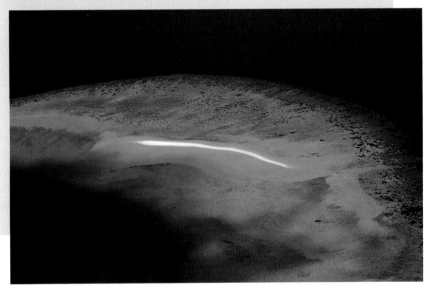

History

Not much is known about the early history of the Maldives. Thor Heyerdahl, the Norwegian explorer, believes the first settlers were sun-worshipping seafarers who settled here as early as 2000 BC. Called the Redin, they left behind a pagan heritage of beliefs and customs that still exist today. Curiously, many mosques in the Maldives are oriented to the sun, not Mecca.

Around 500 BC the Redin either left or were absorbed by Buddhists from Sri Lanka and Hindus from India. Both groups left their mark in temple ruins and linguistic traces.

In the 12th century AD, Arab traders and explorers showed increasing interest in the Maldives, for both its strategic importance and its abundant supply of cowry shells, an international currency of the early ages. Contact with the Arabs eventually led to the conversion of the Maldivian people from Buddhism to Islam. In 1153 a Sunni Muslim, Abu al Barakat, was credited with the conversion of the last Buddhist king of the Maldives. This began a series of six dynasties ruled by 84 sultans and sultanas in all.

The Portuguese arrived in the Maldives in the 16th century. Already well established in Goa, western India, the Portuguese decided they wanted a greater share of the profitable Indian

A pre-Islamic bust of Buddha graces the National Museum.

Ocean trade routes. They were granted permission to build a fort and a factory in Male', but greed soon prevailed. In 1558 Captain Andreas Andre and his army invaded the Maldives, killed Sultan Ali VI and ruled Male' for the next 15 years. Andre's own oppressive reign came to a bloody end, when in 1573 chief Mohammed Thakurufaanu successfully attacked and killed the Portuguese. Thakurufaanu began a new dynasty as sultan.

In the 17th century the Maldives accepted the protection of the Dutch, who ruled Ceylon at the time. The British unofficially assumed the role of protector when they took Ceylon in 1796. Not until 1887 did the British recognize the Maldives' statehood and formalize its protected status.

In 1932 a constitution was imposed to make the sultanate elective. Then in 1953 the sultanate was abolished and a republic was proclaimed, with Amin Didi as its first president. The new government was short-lived, however, as Didi was overthrown and killed less than a year later, leading to the reestablishment of the elective sultanate.

Shortly after being granted independence from Britain in 1965, Maldivians again abolished the sultanate, and a new republic was inaugurated.

In 1988 third-term President Maumoon Abdul Gayoom was the target of a coup attempt by a group of Maldivian businessmen, who employed about 90 Sri Lankan Tamil mercenaries. The attempt failed when Indian Prime Minister Rajiv Gandhi dispatched 1,600 Indian paratroopers to end the coup. The invaders fled by boat, taking 27 hostages and leaving 14 people dead and 40 wounded. No tourists were affected.

Gayoom began his fifth term as president in 1998.

Diving History

In the 1980s, when a tourism master plan was developed for the Maldives, officials played up what they called the "Robinson Crusoe Factor"—appealing to tourists whose vision of paradise comprised unspoiled tropical islands with palm-fringed beaches and turquoise lagoons. It didn't take long to realize that the Maldives' magnificent underwater world was part of the attraction.

In 1972 the first dive school was established at Bandos Island Resort in North Male' Atoll, and Eurodivers soon opened a dive school at Kurumba Village Tourist Resort. Safari dive boats were also quickly on the scene. Vessels such as *Makona* and *Isdhoo* began their cruises in 1972. Rustic by today's standards, these boats offered fishing and cruising tours in addition to live-aboard diving. In 1975 Ahmed Hassan built the first dedicated safari dive boat, *Allaudheen*, which accommodated up to six guests. Since then dozens of resorts and safari dive boats have begun operations, and several outlying atolls have opened to tourism.

Many famous underwater explorers, photographers and filmmakers have visited the Maldives, including Austrian diving pioneer Hans Hass and world famous French explorer Jacques Cousteau. Local legends include Hassan Maniku (nicknamed Lakudiboa), an experienced diver who has taken part in marine projects ranging from deep salvage operations to the exploration of new reefs.

MICHAEL AW

Barutheela is one of many live-aboards in the Maldives.

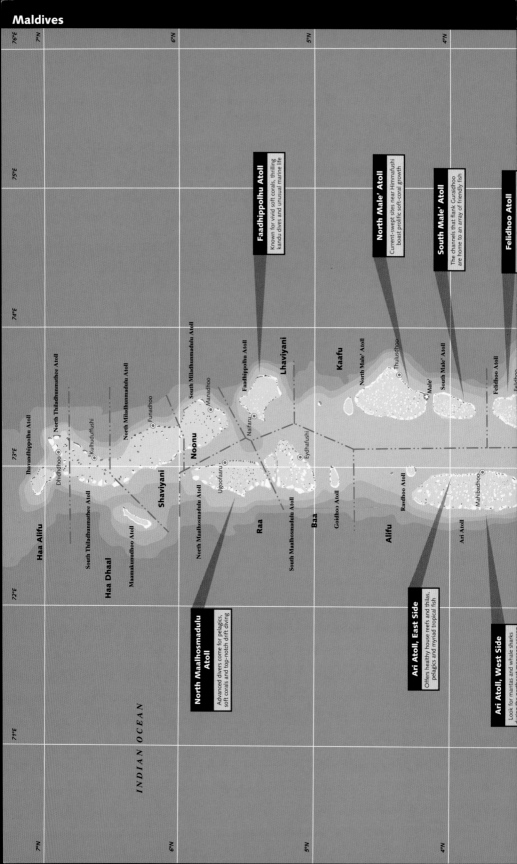

Faadhippolhu Atoll
Known for vivid soft corals, thrilling kandu dives and unusual marine life

North Male' Atoll
Current-swept sites near Himmafushi boast prolific soft-coral growth

South Male' Atoll
The channels that flank Guraidhoo are home to an array of friendly fish

Felidhoo Atoll

North Maalhosmadulu Atoll
Advanced divers come for pelagics, soft corals and top-notch drift diving

Ari Atoll, East Side
Offers healthy house reefs and thilas, pelagics and myriad tropical fish

Ari Atoll, West Side
Look for mantas and whale sharks

INDIAN OCEAN

Ihavandhippolhu Atoll

North Thiladhunmathee Atoll

Haa Alifu

South Thiladhunmathee Atoll

Haa Dhaal

Dhidhdhoo
Kulhudhuffushi

North Miladhunmadulu Atoll

Maamakunudhoo Atoll

Funadhoo

Shaviyani

North Maalhosmadulu Atoll

Noonu

Ugoofaaru

South Maalhosmadulu Atoll

Raa

Baa

Goidhoo Atoll

South Miladhunmadulu Atoll

Manadhoo

Faadhippolhu Atoll

Naifaru

Lhaviyani

Eydhafushi

Alifu

Raadhoo Atoll

Kaafu

North Male' Atoll

Thulusdhoo

'Male'

South Male' Atoll

Ari Atoll

Mahibadhoo

Felidhoo Atoll

Felidhoo

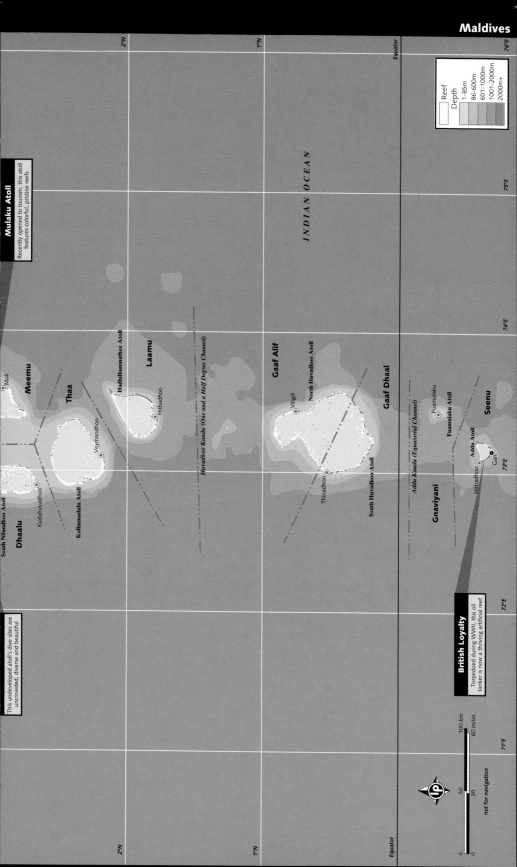

Maldives

Mulaku Atoll
Recently opened to tourism, this atoll features colorful, pristine reefs

This undeveloped atoll's dive sites are uncrowded, diverse and beautiful

South Nilandhoo Atoll

Dhaalu

Kudahuvadhoo

Kolhumadulu Atoll

Meemu
Muli

Thaa
Veymandhoo

Hadhdhunmathee Atoll

Laamu
Hithadhoo

Huvadhoo Kandu (One and a Half Degree Channel)

INDIAN OCEAN

Gaaf Alif
Viligili

North Huvadhoo Atoll

Thinadhoo

South Huvadhoo Atoll

Gaaf Dhaal

Addu Kandu (Equatorial Channel)

Gnaviyani
Fuamulaku

Fuamulaku Atoll

Addu Atoll

Hithadhoo
Gan

Seenu

2°N

1°N

Equator

British Loyalty
Torpedoed during WWII, this oil tanker is now a thriving artificial reef

Reef

Depth
1-85m
86-600m
601-1000m
1001-2000m
2000m+

100 km
60 miles
0
0
50
30
not for navigation

76°E
75°E
74°E
73°E
72°E
71°E

Practicalities

Climate

The Maldives experiences two monsoon seasons—the northeast monsoon (*iruvai*) and the southwest monsoon (*hulhangu*). The northeast monsoon blows from December through March, bringing drier weather and prevailing winds out of the northeast. The soggier southwest monsoon lasts from May to November, with the heaviest rains between June and September. Expect cloudy days, with frequent gales and moderate to rough seas. As the Maldives islands straddle the equator, severe cyclones are extremely rare.

March and April are the hottest months. Mid-April and late November are considered transition periods between monsoons, with sunny, windless days in April and shifting winds in November.

The climate does vary widely between the northern and southern atolls, with more rainfall in the south and greater temperature extremes in the north. However, the average maximum temperature is remarkably consistent throughout the year, ranging from 30 to 32°C (86 to 90°F) during the daytime, while nights are between 25 and 26°C (77 and 79°F).

Water temperatures generally stay between 27 and 30°C (81 and 86°F), although thermoclines sometimes bring slightly cooler water below 20m (65ft).

Language

Saying Hi in Dhivehi

Break the ice by using some useful everyday civilities and diving terms:

Civilities		Diving Terms	
Hi	*Kihine*	*falhu*	lagoon encircled by a reef
Hello	*A-salam alekum*	*faru*	ring-shaped reef facing the ocean
Peace	*Salam*	*finolhu*	small island with sparse vegetation
How are you?	*Haalu kihine?*	*fushi*	larger, vegetated island
OK	*Enge*	*giri*	underwater pinnacle almost reaching the surface
Thank you	*Shukuria*		
See you later	*Fahung badaluvang*	*kandu*	channel
Farewell	*Vale kumu salam*	*mas*	fish
		thila	underwater pinnacle at least 5m (16ft) below the surface

The official language of the Maldives is Dhivehi. Believed to have developed from Sinhala, an ancient Sri Lankan dialect, Dhivehi also contains Arabic, Hindi and even some English words. English is widely spoken in Male', in the tourist resorts and by educated people throughout the country. Many young children also speak and write English, as it's now taught in school. In the resorts and aboard safari dive boats, you'll often find instructors and other staff who speak English, French, German, Spanish, Italian and/or Japanese.

STAEVEN VALLAK
Maldivian schoolchildren learn English at an early age.

The written language, Thaana, runs from right to left, similar to Arabic. As with Arabic, there is no official written translation of Thaana, just various forms of transliteration. Words are spelled a variety of ways. Dhivehi itself is often spelled Divehi. This book uses a set of standardized terms.

Getting There

Nearly everyone who visits the Maldives arrives by air. The occasional cruise ship does stop, but there are no regular passenger boats to or from the country. Although possible, traveling to the Maldives by private yacht is not a very popular option due to the maze of hazardous reefs and the potentially high cruising permit fees.

There is only one international airport in the Maldives, Male' International Airport, on Huhule Island, 2km (1.2 miles) northeast of the capital. While Europeans can visit the Maldives on a variety of charter flights, there are no direct flights from North America. Scheduled commercial carriers include Emirates Airlines, SriLankan Airlines, Indian Airlines and Singapore Airlines, with stopovers in Colombo, Sri Lanka, or Singapore.

Gateway City – Male'

The Maldives' capital, Male' (pronounced MAH-lee) is an unusual city in many ways. Reflecting the country's Muslim culture with its numerous mosques and traditional teahouses, the city encompasses an island only 2km (1.2 miles) long and 1km (.6 mile) wide. Every square foot of the island is used to house the population of at least 65,000 Maldivian residents and approximately 20,000 foreign workers.

One controversial solution to overcrowding is the creation of a new island, Hulhu-Male', a few kilometers northwest. Sand and coral is being dredged from the lagoon and pumped onto the reef to raise it about a meter above sea level, and a number of apartment complexes are planned. Additional growth will only be possible by adding high-rise buildings or spreading development to neighboring islands.

The international airport is on nearby Huhule, and all transfers to Male' are made by boat. Few tourists spend more than a night in Male', hence most hotels cater to the business traveler, with clean, functional rooms.

Why the Apostrophe?

There's some confusion regarding the spelling of Male'. You may also see it written as Malé or simply Male. It was often assumed that Maldivians adopted the apostrophe because they couldn't type an acute accent on early typewriters. Foreign publishers converted the apostrophe to an accent, a practice soon widely adopted. However, the most common local spelling remains with an apostrophe on the end, used because the name is a contraction—it comes from the Malei dynasty, which ruled the Maldives for 160 years from the time of conversion to Islam.

Male'

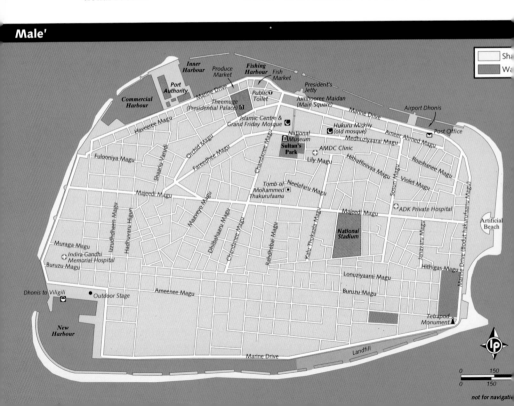

Getting Around

In an attempt to shield Muslim society from Western influences, the Maldivian government requires visitors to obtain an inter-atoll travel permit to visit any island other than Male', Gan or a resort island. You must also have a local sponsor who will guarantee your accommodation. Applications are available at the Ministry of Atolls Administration, on Marine Drive in Male'.

Travel agents and the resorts themselves usually arrange airport transfers, which involve travel by seaplane, local boat (dhoni), speedboat or launch. Scheduled domestic flights link five airfields throughout the country, but only the fields on Huhule and Gan are accessible to visitors without a travel permit.

There are no regular, scheduled ferry links in the Maldives. Visitors may charter a variety of boats and seaplanes, though people rarely travel between resorts. If necessary, it may be easier to return to the Male' airport on the first resort's pre-arranged transfer, then board the other resort's transfer.

Safari dive boats are another popular way to cruise the islands (see Diving in the Maldives, page 34, for more information).

Once you're on an island, the best way to get around is on foot. Even Male' itself is so small that the shops, tourist attractions and downtown are within a few minutes' walk from any of the hotels. Taxis are also available at reasonable rates.

The Maldivian Dhoni

Developed and perfected over centuries to conquer the seas, the dhoni is based on the craftsmanship, ingenuity and art of the carpenter —skills passed from one generation to the next. Steered by rudder with the helmsman's legs, dhonis were traditionally fitted with sails, but over the last few years most have been motorized. A sail may still be used to take advantage of a good breeze on longer journeys.

Raa Atoll is famous for the construction of dhonis, a process that may take several months, as boatbuilders still rely on only a few basic tools. Initially used for fishing, dhonis now also serve as dive boats, interisland transports and water taxis between Male' and the airport.

MICHAEL AW

Entry

All tourists must have a valid passport and an onward or return airline ticket.

Most foreign visitors are given a free 30-day visitor's permit on arrival; citizens of India, Pakistan, Bangladesh and Nepal receive 90-day permits. Extensions for a maximum of 30 additional days are possible, but you must apply at the immigration office in Male'. A representative of your resort or safari boat may be able to arrange the extension for you. Overstaying your original or extended visa can lead to airport hassles and a possible fine.

Maldivian customs laws strictly forbid the import of alcohol, pornography, pork, firearms, spearguns, narcotics and idols of worship such as a crucifix or Buddha statue. Baggage is X-rayed and sometimes thoroughly searched.

Time

The Maldives is five hours ahead of GMT, in the same time zone as Pakistan and only half an hour behind Sri Lanka and India. Daylight saving time is not observed; the rest of the year, when it's noon in the Maldives, it's 5pm in Sydney, 8am in London, 3am in New York and midnight in San Francisco.

Several resorts operate one to two hours ahead of Male' time to allow guests extra daylight in the evening and longer to sleep in the morning.

Money

The Maldivian currency is the rufiya (Rf), which is divided into 100 larees. However, the rufiya is rarely used. Tourist resorts, restaurants and shops not only price everything in U.S. dollars, they may actually refuse to accept rufiya. Accordingly, the best currency to bring with you is the U.S. dollar, though resorts also accept British pounds, Australian dollars, German marks, Japanese yen, Italian lire and French and Swiss francs.

Traveler's checks and credit cards are also widely accepted, though additional fees may apply. The few ATMs in Male' are for Bank of Maldives account holders only.

A 10% service charge may be added to your resort or restaurant bill; if not, it's customary to tip for good service.

Electricity

Although there is no national power grid, Male' has a reliable central electricity supply. All resorts use diesel-powered generators, which usually operate 24 hours a day. Electricity supply ranges from 220 to 240V, 50 Hz AC.

Socket configurations vary, so it's best to bring a multi-socket adapter. Most resorts offer a multiuse socket in the bathroom, which accepts razors using 110V with a variety of pin configurations. While safari dive boats that cater to the U.S. market provide 110V outlets for recharging batteries, etc., the sockets are often not U.S. configured, so you'll still need an adapter.

Weights & Measures

Despite officially converting to the metric system, Maldivians commonly use imperial measures. In this book both metric and imperial measurements are given, except for specific references in dive site descriptions, which are given in metric units only. Please refer to the conversion chart provided on the inside back cover.

What to Bring

General

Wear lightweight, casual clothing that will protect you from insects and sun over-exposure. Bathing suits and short shorts for women are practical and acceptable around resorts and on safari boats but should not be worn in the fishing villages or in Male'. A windbreaker is helpful on rainy or windy days.

It's a good idea to bring plenty of sunscreen and insect repellent, though resorts should have ample supplies of both. Definitely bring all the film and batteries you may need.

Dive-Related

Quality, brand-name rental scuba equipment is available at most dive resorts, though you should inquire ahead of time. Safari dive boats typically only have a limited supply of rental equipment, since divers tend to bring their own.

Underwater, a lycra dive skin is all that's required, mostly to protect yourself from sunburn, coral cuts and abrasions. If you get cold easily, you may want to bring a 3mm suit, especially on rainy days, when it's more difficult to retain your body heat throughout a day of diving.

Underwater Photography

Although the Maldives hosts several underwater photography competitions, there are relatively few processing labs. It's often too expensive and difficult to import and maintain the necessary chemicals. However, some of the dive centers do offer on-site E6 processing, and resorts near Male' can send your film to a professional lab there. This type of service takes about two days.

Few of the safari boats offer E6 on a regular basis, but if an entire group requests the service, it may be possible to hire a professional lab technician who will join the cruise and develop film directly onboard.

Many dive centers rent underwater cameras, usually a variety of Sea & Sea models; inquire in advance to be sure. Most resorts also stock slide and print film, though you should bring your own to ensure it's fresh and the type you need.

Business Hours

Business hours vary and are largely dictated by Islamic traditions.

Banks and government offices are open from 7:30am to 2pm Sunday to Thursday and closed on Friday. Shops have flexible hours, though most open between 7:30 and 9am and wrap things up between 9 and 11pm, closing for an afternoon siesta and during daily prayer calls.

Accommodations

Overall, the Maldives is an expensive destination, and resort pricing structures are complicated. Almost all visitors stay either in a resort or aboard a safari dive boat (see Listings, pages 135-148, for contact information). Resorts are on otherwise uninhabited islands, and standards are typically high. None offers rooms for budget travelers. Safari boats range from rustic to modern and luxurious.

Accommodation options in Male' are quite limited, considering it's the capital, but you will find everything from budget guesthouses and lodges to a few nice hotels.

Stays on locally inhabited islands are strictly governed, requiring both a permit and a local sponsor. Such visits stand on ceremony and require guests to be on their best behavior.

Dining & Food

Maldivian staple foods are rice and fish, including fish patties, fish soup, fish curry and other variations. Meat and chicken are saved for special occasions. Locally grown produce includes coconuts, bananas and breadfruit. Most other

Aside from a few locally grown items such as bananas and coconuts, most food is imported.

foods are imported. Few resorts or safari dive boats serve Maldivian food, apart from a Maldivian barbecue buffet, which is usually quite good.

Thanks to the improved variety of imported items, the food served at resorts and aboard safari boats is often excellent, though the quality of the meals is often tied to the resort rates. Some of the larger resorts have several restaurants and offer a range of European dishes, while resorts far from Male' sometimes have trouble getting fresh supplies. In Male' itself you'll find traditional Maldivian tearooms and modern restaurants that serve European and Asian cuisine, as well as a couple of supermarkets.

Alcohol is not served in Male', unless you are a foreign resident and possess a liquor permit. However, alcohol is available at the resorts and aboard high-end safari boats, though choices are usually limited, and prices are high. Nonalcoholic beer and soft drinks are widely available.

Shopping

Local handicrafts include beautiful lacquerwork, fine woven mats (*kunaa*) from South Huvadhoo Atoll, rosewood carvings, traditional silk dresses (*libaas*) and jewelry made from mother-of-pearl and black coral. Merchants also import a wide range of handicrafts from Sri Lanka, India and Bali, including jewelry, marble products, wood carvings and decorative fans. You'll also find lots of locally made and imported T-shirts, beach towels, colorful wraps and the like.

The best place to shop is Male'. Villages in the tourist atolls have converted their main streets into shopping arcades, selling mostly souvenirs, while the resort shops offer a limited range of souvenirs and imported gifts. Haggling is limited to the village souvenir shops and the Singapore Bazaar in Male'.

The Maldivian government has banned the capture of turtles and the import, export and sale of all turtle-shell products. The import of such products is forbidden to countries that are party to the Convention on International Trade in Endangered Species, including Australia, the U.S. and the member nations of the European Union. It's also forbidden to sell or export any "unfinished" coral and shell products. This means that shells and coral can be used for craft work but cannot be sold in their natural state. Remember, however, that most of these animals are killed for their shells. By buying such souvenirs, you only encourage islanders to collect more live specimens, which can disrupt the ecological balance on the reefs.

Lacquerwork is locally produced.

Activities & Attractions

Renowned among divers and snorkelers worldwide, the Maldives is a haven for any watersports enthusiast. Sailors, surfers, windsurfers and kayakers will have ample opportunities to get out on the water, while anglers will reap a bounty from the sea.

Resorts offer a full range of watersports, as well as topside sports such as tennis, soccer, beach volleyball and badminton. They also arrange island-hopping trips, with snorkeling and lunch on the beach, as well as village visits, for a glimpse at local culture and a chance to pick up souvenirs. (See Listings, pages 139-148, for resort contact information.)

The capital city and cosmopolitan center of the Maldives, Male' boasts such cultural attractions as museums, bustling markets and traditional Maldivian mosques and houses.

Island Hopping & Village Visits

All resorts offer excursions to other islands, usually on half- or full-day dhoni trips. You may visit uninhabited islands for snorkeling, beachcombing and a picnic or barbecue lunch, or visit another resort island, where you can have a drink and enjoy the facilities.

Trips to locally inhabited islands are also possible, though many of the villages near the tourist resorts now comprise rows of souvenir vendors, eagerly selling everything from locally made handicrafts to imported carvings and T-shirts. Safari dive boats sometimes visit the more remote traditional villages.

Male' Walking Tours

Many hotels in Male' offer walking tours led by knowledgeable guides, though it's also possible to take a self-guided walk around the island. Maps from the Maldives Tourism Promotion Board are available at the airport and at their offices in town.

The golden dome of **Grand Friday Mosque** is the most prominent feature in downtown Male'. Flaunting beautifully carved wooden side panels and doors and impressive chandeliers, the main prayer hall can accommodate up to 5,000 worshippers. Visitors are forbidden to enter during prayer times and must dress appropriately (long pants for men and a long skirt or dress for women).

JOHN BORTHWICK

Throughout the Maldives, mosques with lofty minarets proclaim the country's Islamic beliefs.

Dating back to 1656, **Hukuru Miskiiy** is the Maldives' oldest mosque, also known for its intricate carvings. One long panel, carved in the 13th century, commemorates the introduction of Islam to the Maldives.

The **National Museum** is housed in the only remaining part of the original sultan's palace. Most of the exhibits are belongings of the former sultans—clothing, utensils, weapons and a throne. Especially interesting are the pre-Islamic stone carvings collected by Thor Heyerdahl and others.

Surrounding the museum is **Sultan's Park**, once part of the grounds of the sultan's palace.

One Man's House Is Another Man's Leaf Mess

While street names in Male' may not sound familiar, house names are typically in English. Marine titles and anything with the word blue in it are especially popular, such as Sea Speed, Marine Dream, Dawn Dive, Blue Haven and Bright Blue. The tropical sun gives rise to the likes of Sun Dance, Radiant, Sunny Coast and Plain Heat. More obscure choices include Leaf Mess, Mary Lightning and Remind House.

Surfing

The southwest monsoon season (May to November) stirs up the best surf in the Maldives, with prime spots near the tourist resorts. The best breaks are along outer reefs on the southeast sides of the atolls, where channel openings allow the waves to wrap around.

Surfers can either stay in a resort and take a boat to the surf spots or arrange for a live-aboard surfing safari. Surfing season is low season, so accommodations and boats are readily available.

Windsurfing

Many resorts offer windsurfing lessons and rentals. Those particularly known for good windsurfing include **Reethi Rah** in North Male', **Reethi Beach** in South Maalhosmadulu and **Kuramathi** in Rasdhoo Atoll, north of Ari.

Although conditions on the calm lagoons are often ideal for beginners, the many shallow reefs make windsurfing potentially hazardous if you fall. Get proper instruction and be aware of your surroundings.

Kayaking

Available for rent at most resorts, sturdy ocean kayaks are a great way to explore the shallow lagoons and even snorkel while tethered to the kayak. Though trips to other islands are not usually permitted, some operators are exploring the possibility of extended kayak excursions.

Fishing

While spearfishing is forbidden in the Maldives, anglers can choose from a variety of outings. Most resorts organize night fishing trips, done for smaller species with a handline and a bucket of bait. You can usually arrange to have your catch prepared by the resort's chef.

Many anglers prefer traditional Maldivian tuna fishing trips, with a pole, line and unbaited hook. Resorts offering this more authentic experience include **Asdu Sun Island** in North Male' and **Kuredu Island Resort** in Faadhippolhu.

Finally, tag-and-release sportfishing for billfish such as marlin and sailfish is available through **Universal Enterprises** (39 Orchid Magu, Male', ☎ 323080) out of **Baros**, **Full Moon**, **Kurumba** and **Nakatchafushi** resorts in North Male' and **Laguna Beach** resort in South Male'.

Sailing

Most resorts rent catamarans (such as Hobie Cats or Top Cats) for about US$25 per hour, US$40 with lessons. Rentals are cheaper by the day or week.

If you wish to charter a sailing yacht and cruise North and South Male', contact **Sunsail** charter company (☎ 312101, kethi@dhivehinet.net.mv), based at **Giravaru Tourist Resort**, about 11km (7 miles) west of Male'. If you can demonstrate prior experience and/or certification, you can rent your own vessel. Otherwise, you can request a skipper for an extra charge.

For a relaxing ramble at your own pace, rent a catamaran for the day.

MICHAEL AW

Diving Health & Safety

The Maldives has remarkably few health risks, especially on the resort islands and aboard most safari dive boats. Although a few cases of malaria have been reported on some of the outer atolls, the disease is not considered a problem in the tourist atolls. Consider taking a course of antimalarial tablets, though divers may experience adverse reactions. Also consider vaccinations for diphtheria, tetanus, polio, cholera and hepatitis. If you're coming from an area where yellow fever is endemic, you must furnish proof of vaccination.

Divers should be especially wary of health hazards such as sun overexposure, diarrhea and infections from coral cuts. These nuisances are easily avoided or minimized by following a few precautions. Be sure to carry waterproof sunblock and lip balm with you and reapply them frequently. When topside, stay in the shade and drink plenty of fluids.

Avoid drinking untreated water. If you visit a Maldivian village, don't drink the tap water—purchase bottled water instead. In the resorts and aboard safari boats, the tap water is usually desalinated seawater, which is probably safe to drink, though it may taste slightly salty. While rainwater is sometimes available, bottled water is a better option.

Wear an exposure suit while snorkeling to avoid sunburn and while diving to avoid coral cuts. If an injury occurs, no matter how small, be sure to clean and treat the wound immediately. If it becomes necessary to visit a clinic, inform resort management immediately so they can arrange transportation to Male'.

Diving & Flying

Most divers in the Maldives arrive by plane. While it's fine to dive soon *after* flying, it's important to remember that your last dive should be completed at least 24 hours *before* your flight to minimize the risk of decompression sickness, caused by residual nitrogen in the blood.

Pre-Trip Preparation

Your general state of health, diving skill level and specific equipment needs are the three most important factors that impact any dive trip. If you honestly assess these before you leave, you'll be well on your way to assuring a safe dive trip.

First, if you're not in shape, start exercising. Second, if you haven't dived for a while (six months is too long), and your skills are rusty, do a local dive with an experienced buddy or take a scuba review course. Feeling good physically and diving regularly will make you a safer diver and enhance your enjoyment underwater.

At least a month before your trip, inspect your dive gear. Remember, your regulator should be serviced annually, whether you've used it or not. If you use a dive computer and can replace the battery yourself, change it before the trip or buy a spare one to take along. Otherwise, send the computer to the manufacturer for a battery replacement.

If possible, find out if the dive center you'll be using rents or services the type of gear you own. If not, you might want to take spare parts or even spare gear. A spare mask is always a good idea.

Purchase any additional equipment you might need, such as a dive light and tank marker light for night diving, a line reel for wreck diving, etc. Make sure you have at least a whistle attached to your BC. Better yet, add a marker tube (also known as a safety sausage or come-to-me).

Get any immunizations you'll need and fill prescriptions. Certain immunizations and treatments might need to begin several months before you leave.

About a week before taking off, do a final check of your gear, grease o-rings, check batteries and assemble a save-a-dive kit. This kit should at minimum contain spare mask and fin straps, snorkel keeper, mouthpiece, valve cap, zip ties and o-rings. Don't forget to pack a first-aid kit and medications such as decongestants, ear drops, antihistamines and motion sickness tablets.

Tips for Evaluating a Dive Operator

First impressions mean a lot. Does the business appear organized and professionally staffed? Does it prominently display a dive affiliation such as NAUI, PADI, BSAC, SSI, etc.? This is a good indication that it adheres to high standards.

When you arrive, a well-run business will always have paperwork ready for you to fill out. At the least, they should look at your certification card and ask when you last dived. If they want to see your logbook or check basic skills in the water, even better.

Rental equipment should be well rinsed. If you see sand or salt crystals, watch out. Before starting on your dive, inspect the equipment thoroughly: Check the hoses for wear, see that mouthpieces are secure and make sure they've given you a depth gauge and air pressure gauge.

After gearing up and turning on your air, listen for air leaks. Now test your BC: Push the power inflator to make sure it functions correctly (and doesn't free-flow); if it fails, get another BC and don't try to inflate it manually; make sure the BC holds air. Then purge your regulator a bit and smell the air. It should be odorless. If you detect an oily or otherwise bad odor, try a different tank, then start searching for another operator.

DAN

Divers Alert Network (DAN) is an international membership association of individuals and organizations sharing a common interest in diving and safety.

It operates a 24-hour diving emergency hot line in the U.S.: ☎ **919-684-8111** or **919-684-4DAN** (-4326). The latter accepts collect calls in a dive emergency. DAN Maldives, an affiliate of DAN Europe, is a new member of International Divers Alert Network and provides Maldivian national and resident divers, as well as visiting divers, with the full range of DAN benefits and services (☎ 440088).

Though DAN does not directly provide medical care, it does offer advice on early treatment, evacuation, and hyperbaric treatment of diving-related

Tips for Evaluating a Dive Boat

In the Maldives dive boats can be anything from basic dhonis to elegant safari boats. Before departure, take a good look at the vessel. A well-outfitted dive boat has communication with onshore services. It also carries oxygen, a recall device and a first-aid kit. A larger boat should have a shaded area and a supply of fresh drinking water.

A well-prepared crew will give a thorough pre-dive briefing that explains procedures for dealing with an emergency when divers are in the water. The briefing will also explain how divers should enter the water and get back onboard. If the boat ladder looks steep or otherwise challenging, ask if the crew is willing to take your BC and tank from you in the water. When dealing with groups, a good crew will get everyone's name on a dive roster so it can initiate an immediate search if a diver is missing. This is something you should always verify.

In a strong current, the crew might provide a special descent line and should be able to throw out a drift line from the stern. For deep dives the crew should hang a safety tank at 5m (16ft). On night dives a good boat will have powerful lights, including a strobe light.

MICHAEL AW

injuries. Divers should contact DAN for assistance as soon as a diving emergency is suspected.

DAN membership is reasonably priced and includes DAN TravelAssist, a benefit that covers medical air evacuation from anywhere in the world for any illness or injury. For a small additional fee, divers can get secondary insurance coverage for decompression illness. For membership details, contact DAN at ☎ 800-446-2671 in the U.S. or ☎ 919-684-2948 elsewhere. DAN can also be reached at www.diversalertnetwork.org.

Medical & Recompression Facilities

Although it's being continually upgraded, the health care system in the Maldives is limited. There is a government hospital or health center on the capital island of each atoll, but the country's main hospital is Indira Gandhi Memorial Hospital on Male'. Emergency evacuations are coordinated by the National Coast Guard and independent seaplane companies. Patients requiring specialized care must be evacuated to Singapore or Colombo, Sri Lanka.

DAN Europe actively promotes diving safety in the Maldives through its affiliate member DAN Maldives. The organization supports the **Bandos Medical Clinic & Hyperbaric Centre** (☎ 440088, maldives@daneurope.org), capable of treating any level of hyperbaric emergency. The facility is at Bandos Island Resort in North Male'.

Medical Contacts

Patients with serious conditions should go to the following medical facilities in Male'. Contact your resort or safari boat management to arrange the necessary transportation.

Indira Gandhi Memorial Hospital
☎ 316647

AMDC Clinic
☎ 325979

ADK Private Hospital
☎ 313553

JAMES LYON

Diving in the Maldives

Maldives diving is truly unique, offering perhaps the very best fish-watching and photo opportunities in the world. Schooling tropicals, roaming pelagics and sea turtles are abundant and often easily approached. The sites themselves are riddled with caves, caverns, overhangs, arches, windows or a combination of each. These fascinating formations are often packed with colorful marine life, such as crimson soldierfish, vivid coral hinds and brilliant soft corals. But divers often overlook this magnificent spectacle of color, as it gets quite dark beneath the formations, and colors are quickly absorbed. Don't miss out—carry at least a small dive light on all dives. Photographers should mount a spotter light on their rig.

All resort islands feature on-site dive centers, which serve as training facilities and bases for daytrip dive boats. Dozens of safari dive boats (live-aboards) also visit sites throughout the Maldives.

Most of the best dive sites are in the channels (kandus) between the open ocean and protected lagoons. Some are wide channels that may feature a pinnacle (thila or giri), offering several dive sites; others are narrow channels easily covered in one dive. Currents here can be quite strong and unpredictable, hence most sites are approached as drift dives from a support vessel for reasons of safety and convenience.

Currents are the lifeblood of the reef, providing nutrients to corals and reef fish and initiating the food chain. When a current is running, soft corals pump themselves up to their fullest, while basslets and other reef fish rise up from the protective reef into the water column to feed, in turn attracting jacks, trevallies, barracuda and other pelagics looking to snack on the reef fish. At the end of the food chain, sharks patiently patrol the reef, stalking the pelagics.

Safari Dive Boats

While daytrip boats visit many of the region's dive sites, some of the more remote reefs are only accessible by safari dive boats, also known as live-aboards. Completely self-contained, these vessels minimize travel time to the sites, allowing divers to maximize their time underwater. Some may be former fishing vessels or other converted boats, while others are purpose-built for diving. Size, amenities, passenger capacity and quality of service vary greatly and may change with ownership of the vessel, so be sure to do your research thoroughly before you commit (see Listings, pages 135-139, for more information). Due to the shallow

Something for Everyone

Dive sites in the Maldives fall under one of the following five categories:

Wreck Dives Considering the Maldives' innumerable shallow reefs and narrow channels, it's likely that shipwrecks have been a fact of life here since ships first arrived in the region. Just off the tourist atolls lie a number of accessible wrecks, ranging from scattered remains of 19th century steamships to perfectly intact modern-day vessels. Many wrecks lie near channel entrances and are swept by strong currents.

Kandu Dives Kandu means channel in the Dhivehi language (see "Say Hi in Dhivehi," page 18). Divers typically enter the channel on the outer lip and drift into the lagoon. Occasionally (more so during the southwest monsoon season), divers approach the channel from the inside out. Kandu dives generally take in only one side of the channel, though divers may cross narrow channels if currents allow. Highlights include pelagic action, schooling fish, caves and soft-coral blooms.

Thila Dives Thila is the Dhivehi word for an underwater pinnacle that tops out at about 5m (16ft) or deeper. Thila dives may be in or near a channel, but revolve around the thila. Other thilas are inside the atolls, protected from currents. Thila dives offer outstanding coral growth, overhangs, schooling reef fish and interesting macro life.

Giri Dives Giri is the Dhivehi word for an underwater pinnacle that tops out just below the surface. Giris of various sizes sit inside many of the atolls, protected from strong currents and swells. These are often easy dives, suitable for novice divers, night dives and macrophotography, though visibility is sometimes only average. Other giris sit within or near the channels, which means conditions similar to kandu dives. Since the water was warmest inside the atolls during the 1998 El Niño, coral bleaching hit the shallow giri reeftops particularly hard. And since nutrient-rich currents don't flush the giris as thoroughly as sites facing the open ocean, the coral is taking longer to recover. Nevertheless, many of these inner lagoon sites are still extremely "fishy" and worth a visit.

House Reef Dives If a resort beach extends directly onto a reef, it's referred to as a house reef. Most house reefs are diveable from shore, though some require a boat transfer. Most are also protected from currents, hence suitable for novices and night divers. Many house reefs are also excellent macro dives. The quality of house reefs varies. Some feature abundant coral, interesting caves and schooling fish. Others are perhaps less exciting, but still make for a relaxing afternoon dive or the ideal setting for a resort course.

EDWARD SNIJDERS

reef formations throughout the archipelago, safari boats do not travel at night in the Maldives.

Smaller safari vessels, those carrying a maximum of six passengers, may drop you off and pick you up at the dive site directly. Larger boats, however, should and usually do use support vessels to shuttle divers to and from the sites. In most cases, these support vessels are dhonis, which carry all the diving gear and travel independently when moving between sites and even atolls.

Almost all safari dive boats leave from Male', though it's often possible to join or start a tour in a different atoll, particularly on chartered trips. Vessel itineraries vary with weather conditions, the length of the charter and customers' desires. Most operators can and will visit any of the tourist atolls (again depending on the weather, length of the charter and the prearranged logistics). The most frequented atolls are Felidhoo, South Male', North Male' and Ari, due to their proximity to Male'.

Safari boats are a comfortable, efficient way to reach dive sites.

Daytrip Dive Boats

Daytrip dive boats are either speedboats or local dhonis. Both have their advantages. Speedboats are obviously faster and cut down on the time it takes to reach the sites; some are custom-built for diving. On the other hand, local boat drivers tend to be more familiar with dhonis, which are quite seaworthy and generally easier to repair.

Snorkeling

The Maldives has long been known for excellent snorkeling. Unfortunately, coral bleaching has significantly damaged the shallow reefs, which is particularly evident while snorkeling. However, there's still plenty here for snorkelers to enjoy, as fish life thrives while the reefs slowly recover.

All resorts offer snorkeling, on either their house reef or organized boat excursions. Those seeking unlimited snorkeling should choose a resort island with an easily accessible house reef. Snorkeling in areas prone to currents may be possible if you are an experienced snorkeler and use a dhoni for drop-off and pickup.

Snorkeling is a perfectly safe activity, provided you follow a few basic precautions. Always notify someone when and where you will be snorkeling and do not snorkel alone. Wear a colorful mask, snorkel and fins, as well as a T-shirt or dive skin, for added visibility at the surface. Carry a safety sausage and storm whistle in case weather conditions suddenly worsen. Only snorkel in current-swept areas when surface conditions are calm—wind chop and large swells can make snorkeling a very uncomfortable if not dangerous experience.

Though damaged by coral bleaching, the shallow reefs are still home to myriad colorful fish.

Dive Training & Certification

The Maldives is a perfect starting point for new divers, as the clear, warm water in the shallow lagoons is a forgiving training environment. All resorts have dive schools that offer courses for beginners and employ qualified PADI, NAUI, SSI or CMAS instructors, many of them competent in several languages.

Just about anyone in reasonably good health can venture underwater on scuba. Some dive organizations offer pool-only scuba programs for children 8 to 11 years old. For people aged 12 and up, beginner programs such as the popular "resort course" start you in either the pool or in the calm shallow lagoon just off the beach. Upon successful completion of this confined water session, you'll be qualified to dive with a professional instructor for the duration of your holiday. The dives and any accomplished skills may be credited toward your Open Water certification (as long as you complete certification within 12 months).

If you choose to enroll in an Open Water course while in the Maldives, count on it taking about five days, including classroom lectures and confined and open water training. Expect to pay about US$400.

Another popular option is the Open Water referral program. You complete your pool and classroom sessions at a dive center near your home, then conduct the open water dives in the Maldives. There are some restrictions and time limits, so be sure to get specifics from both your local dive shop and the Maldives dive center well ahead of time.

Many of the resort-based dive centers also offer a variety of advanced and specialty dive courses such as nitrox or shark diving.

Dive Site Icons

The symbols at the beginning of each dive site description provide a quick summary of some of the important characteristics of each site:

 Good snorkeling or free-diving site.

 Remains or partial remains of a wreck can be seen at this site.

 Sheer wall or drop-off.

 Deep dive. Features of this dive are found in water deeper than 27m (90ft).

 Strong currents may be encountered at this site.

 Strong surge (the horizontal movement of water caused by waves) may be encountered at this site.

 Drift dive. Because of strong currents and/or difficulty in anchoring, a drift dive is recommended at this site.

 Shore dive. This site can be accessed from shore.

 Caves or caverns are a prominent feature of this site. Only experienced cave divers should explore inner cave areas.

 Marine preserve. Special protective regulations apply in this area.

Pisces Rating System for Dives & Divers

The dive sites in this book are rated according to the following diver skill-level rating system. These are not absolute ratings but apply to divers at a particular time, diving at a particular place. For instance, someone unfamiliar with prevailing conditions might be considered a novice diver at one dive area, but an intermediate diver at another, more familiar location.

Novice: A novice diver should be accompanied by an instructor, divemaster or advanced diver on all dives. A novice diver generally fits the following profile:
◆ basic scuba certification from an internationally recognized certifying agency
◆ dives infrequently (less than one trip a year)
◆ logged fewer than 25 total dives
◆ little or no experience diving in similar waters and conditions
◆ dives no deeper than 18m (60ft)

Intermediate: An intermediate diver generally fits the following profile:
◆ may have participated in some form of continuing diver education
◆ logged between 25 and 100 dives
◆ dives no deeper than 40m (130ft)
◆ has been diving in similar waters and conditions within the last six months

Advanced: An advanced diver generally fits the following profile:
◆ advanced certification
◆ has been diving for more than two years and logged over 100 dives
◆ has been diving in similar waters and conditions within the last six months

Regardless of your skill level, you should be in good physical condition and know your limitations. If you are uncertain of your own level of expertise for a particular site, ask the advice of a local dive instructor. He or she is best qualified to assess your abilities based on the site's prevailing dive conditions. Ultimately, however, you must decide if you are capable of making a particular dive, a decision that should take into account your level of training, recent experience and physical condition, as well as the conditions at the site. Remember that conditions can change at any time, even during a dive.

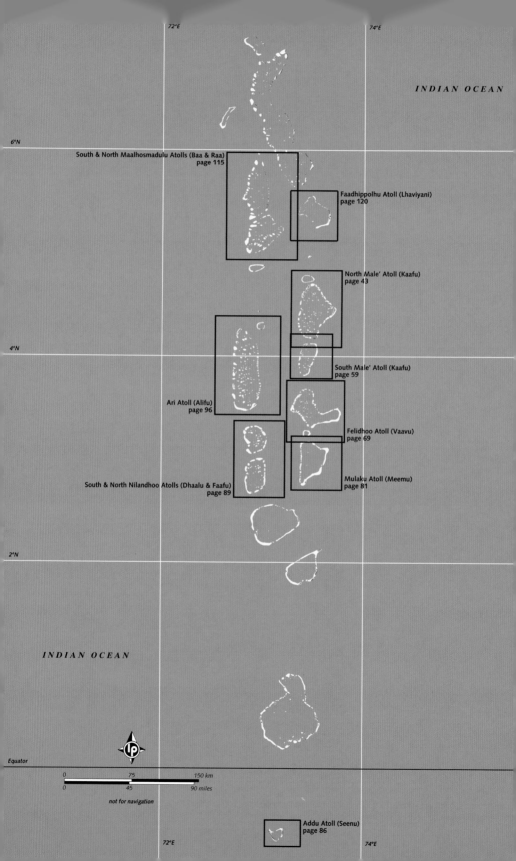

INDIAN OCEAN

6°N

South & North Maalhosmadulu Atolls (Baa & Raa)
page 115

Faadhippolhu Atoll (Lhaviyani)
page 120

North Male' Atoll (Kaafu)
page 43

4°N

South Male' Atoll (Kaafu)
page 59

Ari Atoll (Alifu)
page 96

Felidhoo Atoll (Vaavu)
page 69

Mulaku Atoll (Meemu)
page 81

South & North Nilandhoo Atolls (Dhaalu & Faafu)
page 89

2°N

INDIAN OCEAN

Equator

0   75   150 km
0   45   90 miles

not for navigation

Addu Atoll (Seenu)
page 86

72°E

74°E

North Male' Atoll (Kaafu) Dive Sites

North Male' is home to the Maldives' capital, Male', as well as the country's only international airport, on neighboring Huhule. North Male' was the first atoll to open to tourism and boasts the largest grouping of resort islands and established dive sites in the country. While the atoll shares the same administrative district (Kaafu) as South Male', they are considered separate dive regions. The capital itself is governed under its own administration.

There are seven locally inhabited islands in this atoll, including Male' and Thulusdhoo (the atoll's administrative capital), a couple of traditional fishing islands and a few former fishing islands whose residents now sell handicrafts and souvenirs to tourists. Few truly uninhabited islands remain. Most of the others have been developed into resorts, leased to commercial ventures or used as military camps, garbage dumps, prisons or for other purposes.

JAMES LYON

Everything screeches to a halt during prayer time in Male', the capital city of the Maldives.

41

In spite of the development and high number of visitors in North Male', most of the diving remains excellent. The greatest concentration of dive sites is in the southern half of the atoll, predictably close to the resorts. Although there are some good dive sites near Male', the area is plagued by heavy boat traffic and pollution. There are far fewer resorts in the northern half of the atoll, resulting in less frequented, more remote dive sites.

At the north tip of the atoll, the channel between Gaafaru Falhu and Kaashidhoo is one of the main shipping routes in the Maldives. When negotiating the channel, several ships that drifted too far south ran aground on Gaafaru Falhu and are now thriving artificial reefs. North Male' also offers several exhilarating kandu dives and colorful thilas.

North Male' Atoll (Kaafu) Dive Sites

	Good Snorkeling	Novice	Intermediate	Advanced
1 Lady Christine				●
2 Seagull		●		●
3 Helengeli Thila			●	
4 Fairytale Reef			●	
5 Miyaru Faru			●	
6 Asdu Rock	●	●		
7 Kani Corner			●	
8 HP Reef (Rainbow Reef, Girifushi Thila)				●
9 Okobe Thila (Barracuda Giri)		●		
10 Nassimo Thila (Paradise Rock)				●
11 Manta Point			●	
12 Hannes Reef	●	●		
13 Banana Reef		●		●
14 Maldive Victory				●
15 Hans Hass Place	●	●		
16 Lion's Head	●		●	
17 Hembadhoo Wreck		●		

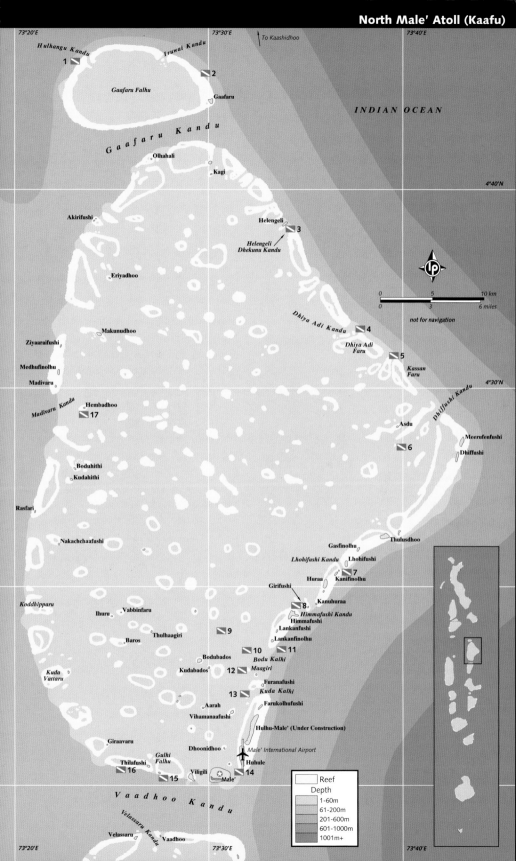

1 Lady Christine

In 1974 this survey vessel ran into the reef about 300m west of Hulhangu Kandu. The wreckage is now scattered, with some pieces fairly shallow along the reef slope and parts of the bow visible above the surface.

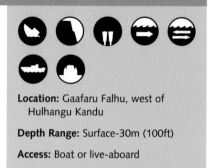

Location: Gaafaru Falhu, west of Hulhangu Kandu

Depth Range: Surface-30m (100ft)

Access: Boat or live-aboard

Expertise Rating: Advanced

The reef drops steeply to 50m, and all along this current-swept wall you'll find bits and pieces of the wreck, which shelter a great variety of marine life. You may spot several species of shrimp, vibrant flatworms and nudibranchs,

Vivid nudibranchs roam the hull of the wreck.

moray eels, adult and juvenile boxfish, puffers, parrotfish and butterflyfish. Stingrays and nurse sharks sometimes visit two beautiful caves at 30m, both of which are profusely decorated with sea fans and soft-coral trees.

This site experiences both superb visibility and very strong currents on a regular basis, so be sure to watch your depth and air supply. During the southwest monsoon season the site is extremely exposed, and large swells can make surface logistics extremely challenging and generate strong surge.

2 Seagull

Carrying three passengers and a crew of 32, the steamship *Seagull* ran aground and sank off Gaafaru Falhu in 1879. The wreck is well broken up and overgrown with coral, though some parts are still recognizable. Debate surrounds the identity of the wreck, but research by German author Claus-Peter Stoll suggests this is its likely resting place.

Location: East side of Gaafaru Falhu

Depth Range: 3-40m (10-130ft)

Access: Boat or live-aboard

Expertise Rating: Advanced

The anchor and other remains lie scattered atop the reef, only a few meters deep. From the reeftop a wall drops to 30m, then slopes less severely. Leaning vertically against this wall is the wreck, now reduced to engine parts and the ribs.

The site is a good macro dive, with plenty of blennies, gobies and nudibranchs living amid the wreckage. You can also explore a nearby cave. Be aware that currents may be quite strong, especially during the northeast monsoon season.

3 Helengeli Thila

Almost 200m long, this oval thila offers an overwhelming abundance of marine life. At 25m and below, the sheer northwest side is honeycombed with caves and overhangs, all beautifully embellished with colorful soft corals, black coral trees, sea fans and lots of fish. If you glance over your shoulder into the blue, you're likely to see pelagics cruising by. Divers frequently spot eagle rays, reef sharks, tuna and jacks in this area. If the current permits, spend as much time here as you can.

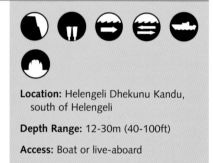

Location: Helengeli Dhekunu Kandu, south of Helengeli

Depth Range: 12-30m (40-100ft)

Access: Boat or live-aboard

Expertise Rating: Intermediate

On the south side of the thila, at 20m, you'll come across a coral-encrusted anchor. While it's an interesting photo subject, nobody is sure of its origin. From here make your way up toward the reeftop, where you'll be greeted by all kinds of tropical reef fish. Juvenile snappers, powder-blue surgeonfish, yellowhead butterflyfish, masked banerfish, parrotfish and wrasses mingle among the branches of the recovering hard-coral reef, as does the occasional massive grouper. Look for scorpionfish on the rubble bottom.

Currents are at times very strong in the channel, and it's best to wait for more moderate conditions when diving the thila, as you may get swept off the site.

EDWARD SNIJDERS

Patrolling the reeftop for its next meal, this brown-marbled grouper may reach lengths up to 90cm.

4   Fairytale Reef

On the south side of Dhiya Adi Kandu, Fairytale Reef is an underwater photographer's dream. At 12m and below, the channel boasts huge, long overhangs filled with squirrelfish, soldierfish, oriental sweetlips, angelfish and many other brightly colored tropicals. The ceilings are decorated with exquisite blue and yellow soft-coral bushes and clusters of tubastrea coral. Amid this profusion of color you may also find small creatures such as brilliant flatworms and nudibranchs, as well as tiny gobies and blennies. The sandy bottom often serves as a resting spot for stingrays and whitetip reef sharks.

Location: South side of Dhiya Adi Kandu

Depth Range: 10-40m (33-130ft)

Access: Boat or live-aboard

Expertise Rating: Intermediate

The outer corner of the channel is a great spot to see mantas during the southwest monsoon season. The mantas are best observed as they pause to benefit from the services of cleaner wrasses.

Colorful soft corals line the overhangs, which shelter squirrelfish, butterflyfish and other reef species.

A Wide-Eyed Look at the Reef

Shooting wide-angle images of the Maldives' colorful reefs can be both rewarding and extremely challenging. Rewarding when you're able to capture the profusion of lush soft corals and brilliant tropical fish. Challenging when you're dealing with currents, contrasty light conditions and extreme color variations.

To succeed, you should read up on the subject, take classes and practice a lot. Here a few Maldives-specific tips to get you started:

First, you must learn to identify colors underwater. All of us remember from our Open Water class that colors are absorbed by water at depth (ROYGBIV, anyone?). Yet underwater photographers frequently miss out on gorgeous wide-angle shots because the crimson reds, oranges, pinks and purples instead appear a boring gray, brown or black at depth. In the Maldives, areas damaged by coral bleaching may look drab but are often coated in a kaleidoscope of sponges and tunicates. Bring along a dive light to appreciate the colors.

Next, you'll have to learn how to deal with currents. Some of the best sites for wide-angle photos are where the current is strongest. There's little chance to shoot a great image when you're exhausting yourself in a current or struggling to keep your strobes in place. Your best bet is to choose a spot where you can get out of the current, dig yourself into the rubble or latch onto a rock or dead piece of coral.

Now you'll have to light up the scene and balance the light. Use two strobes, each aimed at the specific subjects they are to light up. If pink soft corals dominate one side of your frame, while a dark grouper fills the other side, you'll have to adjust your strobes accordingly. As the pale soft coral will reflect more light, adjust that strobe to half or quarter power to avoid overexposure. The darker grouper will absorb light, so you'll probably have to shoot full power, depending on your depth, etc. Of course, you'll want to bracket both your exposures and strobe settings. As the soft corals, reef walls and overhang ceilings are quite reflective in the Maldives, try stopping down an f-stop and turning your strobes to half power.

If you want to include the sun in your image or capture basslets swarming amid the coral, you'll need to set a shutter speed of at least 1/125th of a second.

As far as equipment is concerned, images of equal quality are possible using both housed cameras with an 18 or 20mm lens and Nikonos V cameras fitted with a 15mm lens. Most underwater photographers choose their camera setup based on personal preference and budget.

5 Miyaru Faru

This site is popular with divers who love watching pelagics. *Miyaru* is the Dhivehi word for shark, and this is indeed an excellent place to find grey reef sharks. On the southeast corner of Dhiya Adi Faru, a large overhang at 30m allows divers a place to shelter from the current while taking in the action. Visibility is best with an incoming current, greatly increasing your chances to see the big boys. Besides a number of grey reef sharks, you're likely to spot jacks, barracuda, kingfish, tuna and possibly eagle rays.

From here you can head back to the shallow reeftop or, if the current allows, make your way to a long thila in the mid-

Location: Between Dhiya Adi Faru and Kassan Faru

Depth Range: 3-30m (10-100ft)

Access: Boat or live-aboard

Expertise Rating: Intermediate

dle of the channel. Surrounding the thila are a number of coral pinnacles that attract myriad butterflyfish, parrotfish and groupers. Napoleonfish often visit the thila, while a school of powder-blue surgeonfish grazes its reeftop.

6 Asdu Rock

This large reef formation starts just below the surface and slopes gently to 25m. Its

Location: Inside atoll, south of Asdu

Depth Range: 3-25m (10-82ft)

Access: Boat or live-aboard

Expertise Rating: Novice

Nocturnal glassfish (sweepers) fill the crevices.

protected location inside the atoll shields it from strong currents and large swells, making this spot ideal for snorkelers, novice divers and macrophotographers.

Countless nooks and a number of larger overhangs cradle lots of marine life. Look for glassfish, gobies, juvenile boxfish, triggerfish and filefish, as well as shells, shrimp and morays. To the north, at 25m, a ridge extends from the formation for another 100m, featuring two chimney-like pinnacles and several coral heads that shelter bluelined and humpback snappers.

Coral bleaching has taken its toll on the shallow reeftop, but there are plenty of reef fish, including parrotfish, long-nosed butterflyfish and grazing tangs, while turtles and octopuses are frequent visitors.

7 Kani Corner

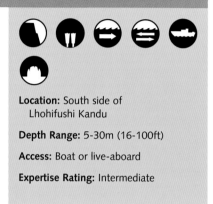

On the sloping corner of Lhohifushi Kandu, just east of Kanifinolhu, this is an excellent site to observe pelagics and schooling fish. The best time to dive here is during the northeast monsoon season, when currents flow mainly into the atoll.

Location: South side of Lhohifushi Kandu

Depth Range: 5-30m (16-100ft)

Access: Boat or live-aboard

Expertise Rating: Intermediate

Enter the water on the outside reef and head toward the channel entrance, dropping down close to where the wall meets a sandy slope at 30m. This is the best area for pelagic encounters. Divers often find large schools of eagle rays, along with sharks, tuna and barracuda. During the southwest monsoon season, you're likely to spot manta rays.

Near the channel entrance, look for the resident Napoleonfish and schooling black-and-white snappers and jacks. The sloping corner features small coral heads where schooling oriental sweetlips swim amid colorful soft corals, offering fantastic photo opportunities. In the channel itself, soldierfish and groupers seek shelter in caves and overhangs that pepper the steep walls.

Strong currents rip through this narrow channel, sometimes spawning hazardous whirlpools. During the southwest monsoon season, when lagoon water flows out of the channel, stay close to the reef and don't let the currents sweep you out to sea.

Strong currents force this school of oriental sweetlips to hug the channel wall.

8 HP Reef (Rainbow Reef, Girifushi Thila)

Lying within Himmafushi Kandu, this protected site is certainly one of the most colorful dives in the Maldives, with an overwhelming density and splendor of soft corals. The dive centers on a thila composed of huge boulder slabs, though most of the highlights are fairly shallow.

The entire southwest side of the thila features outcrops laced with caves, overhangs and swim-throughs. One large cave is adorned with blue, yellow and orange corals, with a chimney that drops from the reeftop to 25m. The overhangs shelter an abundance of black coral trees, sea fans and whip corals, and the outcrops are lavishly festooned with vivid corals in every imaginable hue. Hard-coral gardens in the shallows are partially overgrown with lavender and red sponges and millions of tunicates.

The fish life is just as dazzling as the coral growth. Watch for schools of jacks, black-and-white snappers and sleek

Location: Between Girifushi and Himmafushi

Depth Range: 10-30m (33-100ft)

Access: Boat or live-aboard

Expertise Rating: Advanced

unicornfish. You may also spot eagle rays, barracuda or perhaps reef sharks. Collared butterflyfish, masked bannerfish, and blue-face and three-spot angelfish dart atop the coral-wreathed thila, while lionfish, yellowmouth morays and boxfish also make an appearance.

Currents can be strong here, so duck in and out of the rock formations for shelter. There's an army training camp on nearby Girifushi, and when rifle exercises take place, diving is prohibited—look for the red flag flying from shore.

The thila is blanketed in a kaleidoscope of soft corals—perfect hunting grounds for venomous lionfish.

9 | Okobe Thila (Barracuda Giri)

A variety of dive plans are possible at this extraordinary thila, and despite occasional currents and surge, the site is fine for novices if performed according to one's ability.

Many boats tie up to a hole in the reef at 12m, making it easy to descend, ascend and perform your safety stop. If you plan to return up the line to complete your dive, allow ample time to find your way back to this hole.

The reeftop has suffered some coral bleaching, but Mother Nature has cloaked the damaged coral with crimson and violet sponges. The thila itself comprises three sections, starting at 10m and sloping to about 25m. All sections are carpeted in soft corals and sea fans and punctuated with countless windows, overhangs, nooks and crannies of all sizes. Be sure to bring your dive light and look among these formations for soldierfish, squirrelfish, sweetlips, angelfish and morays.

Several extremely friendly and photogenic Napoleonfish reside here. One of them is humongous, featuring the characteristic hump on its head. You'll also find lionfish, scorpionfish and small schools of batfish, while hundreds of bannerfish hover in the water column just off the thila.

The site is also approached as a drift dive, allowing more flexibility, but making the dive slightly more challenging. From the thila you swim north,

Location: Inside atoll, west of Lankanfushi

Depth Range: 5-25m (16-82ft)

Access: Boat or live-aboard

Expertise Rating: Novice

crossing a sand channel till you reach a long reef that climbs all the way to 5m. Continue north and you'll find countless anemones, their silky undersides boasting such rich colors as blood red, fuchsia and peach. At dusk the anemones ball up, flaunting these brilliant hues. For the best possible photograph, pick one that houses at least a couple of anemonefish.

The reef is also lush with soft corals, encrusting sponges, thousands of tunicates and lots of fish. You'll find schools of collared butterflyfish, phantom and masked bannerfish, glassfish, soldierfish and bluelined snappers, as well as scorpionfish, giant and blackcheek morays and clouds of swirling fusiliers.

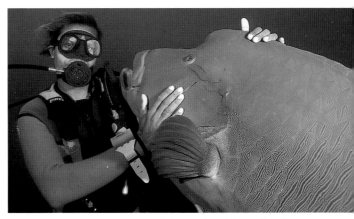

Don't grab—but don't be surprised if a Napoleonfish gets friendly.

10 Nassimo Thila (Paradise Rock)

Swept by currents that press through Bodu Kalhi, this large oval thila boasts incredible diving, particularly on its east side, which faces the ocean. The entire region is alive with a magnificent array of reef fish such as Napoleonfish, emperor angelfish, schools of bluelined snappers, butterflyfish, coral hinds and marbled groupers, to name just a few. Due to its proximity to Paradise Island resort, the site is also known as Paradise Rock.

A large section of the thila has broken off, splintering into pinnacles that reach from the sandy seafloor at 45m to about 20m. Carved with numerous overhangs, these pinnacles are fully exposed to the nutrient-rich ocean currents and are carpeted with multihued soft corals. Swirling above the pinnacles are barracuda, jacks and black-and-white snappers. Where the thila split, the rock is pitted with caves and huge undercuts.

Location: West of Lankanfinolhu

Depth Range: 5-40m (16-130ft)

Access: Boat or live-aboard

Expertise Rating: Advanced

The formations' north face is adorned with a delicate blanket of violet-blue soft corals and colorful encrusting sponges. Packed with long-jawed squirrelfish, oriental sweetlips, anthias and moray eels, this section is a favorite with photographers. Broad gorgonian sea fans, black coral trees and crinoids mark the southeast side of the thila.

Currents here can be treacherous, and most highlights are relatively deep. Wait for a moderate current before diving and reserve plenty of air for your safety stop.

11 Manta Point

This site is famous for the many manta ray encounters divers have logged here,

Location: SE of Lankanfinolhu

Depth Range: 5-40m (16-130ft)

Access: Boat or live-aboard

Expertise Rating: Intermediate

Mantas visit the cleaning stations at this site.

especially during the southwest monsoon season. Shallow coral rocks rise from the reef slope, serving as cleaner stations for these graceful giants. Mantas come in from the deep, then circle or hover "in line" to benefit from the services cleaner wrasses provide. These busy little fish pluck parasites and dead skin cells off the grateful mantas. Patient divers who remain quiet and don't touch or swim after the mantas are often able to observe this ritual up close.

The site offers many other highlights. The reef wall is home to oriental sweetlips, friendly Napoleonfish and several hawksbill turtles, while whitetip reef sharks frequent a large sandy section at about 20m, just south of the cleaning stations. Look for honeycomb morays and octopuses on the open reef, and scan the blue water for barracuda or jacks. At the southwest tip you can explore a series of large caves at various depths. Many of them are elaborately embellished with powder-blue soft corals, sea fans and wire corals. Lionfish, marbled groupers and other species often hide out in the dark recesses.

12 Hannes Reef

Shielded from strong currents and swells, Hannes Reef is an excellent year-round dive—though with a diameter of less than 50m, it can get a bit crowded. This thila is especially popular with macro-photographers and those who appreciate small and unusual critters. The site is also suitable for new divers. Dhoni drivers tie up to a hole in the reeftop at 5m.

Schools of bluelined snappers congregate around the thila, and you'll spot most of the common reef fish throughout the dive. But you'll also find the unusual if you look carefully. Delicate pipefish are common here, as are juvenile yellow boxfish, dragon wrasses and juvenile clown triggerfish. Numerous nooks shelter tiny gobies, banded cleaner shrimp, cowries, nudibranchs and flatworms.

Rare blue-and-yellow ribbon eels are also among the thila's residents, along with masterfully camouflaged stonefish and delicate leaf scorpionfish. At the deeper end of the thila you'll find a couple of caves that house several magnificent lionfish.

Also worth a look, the channel between the thila and Maagiri reef is home to thousands of spotted garden eels, as well as shrimp gobies, sandperch and unusual species of nudibranchs.

Location: West of Maagiri reef

Depth Range: 5-30m (16-100ft)

Access: Boat or live-aboard

Expertise Rating: Novice

Adult male ribbon eels are blue and yellow.

13 Banana Reef

About 300m long, this protected reef is indeed shaped like a banana. Due to its location near Male', the airport and Club Med, Banana Reef was one of the first sites discovered some 20 years ago and has remained one of the prime dive sites in the Maldives. The profusion of color and marine life comes with a price: Currents can be extremely strong and tricky.

Location: West of Kuda Kalhi

Depth Range: 3-30m (10-100ft)

Access: Boat or live-aboard

Expertise Rating: Advanced

The most spectacular area is to the northeast, where part of the reef has broken off. Huge rocks lie scattered along the sloping seafloor, while the main reef is carved with canyons, caves and spectacular overhangs between 10 and 25m. These formations, the rocks and the reef wall are decorated with sea fans, crinoids and soft-coral trees and are thick with long-jawed squirrelfish, coral hinds, moray eels, giant groupers, bluelined snappers and angelfish. Oriental sweetlips and pelagics such as jacks, barracuda, fusiliers and snappers congregate around the rocks, and a vast school of bannerfish inhabits the easternmost point of the reef, showing no fear whatsoever of scuba divers.

Farther west the reef drops to about 30m, adopting a semicircular shape, a feature often referred to as "The Banana." A large overhang reaches from 10 to 15m and is packed with soldierfish.

From here on, the area is known as "The Washing Machine," after whirling currents that are known to pull divers down to 30m and below. To gauge the current, watch your own bubbles or, better yet, those of the diver ahead of you. If the bubbles are going down instead of up, you're caught in a down-current and should respond calmly and deliberately. Stay as close as possible to the reef wall and don't allow the current to sweep you out to sea. After a short while, you should be able to escape the down-current, often finding a corresponding up-current to carry you back to the surface. Be sure to carry a signaling device with you, in the event you do get washed off the reef.

Bannerfish frequent the easternmost point.

14 | *Maldive Victory*

In February 1981 this 3,500-ton freighter was cruising from Singapore to Male', her holds packed with supplies for the resort islands. On Friday the 13th, in the early morning hours, she ran aground at full speed off Huhule, apparently due to a navigational error. The 10-year-old freighter sank surprisingly quickly, though the crew and passengers were all able to make their way safely to the airport landing strip. Local divers and diving instructors mounted an extensive salvage operation, but salt water quickly ruined the various food items, bottles of wine and automobiles.

Location: Directly west of Male' International Airport

Depth Range: 15-35m (50-115ft)

Access: Boat or live-aboard

Expertise Rating: Advanced

Today the wreck rests upright on the sand in 35m of water. Dive boats tie up to a mooring buoy attached to the mast. Napoleonfish, large puffers, batfish, smoke angelfish, collared butterflyfish and lots of nudibranchs are among the wreck's more interesting residents.

Divers usually descend the mooring line to the mast, as currents are sometimes treacherous between Male' and Huhule. If a current is running, continue down the mast to the deck at 25m, where you'll find plenty of shelter from the current. The channel experiences heavy boat traffic, so avoid drifting off the wreck.

From amidships make your way to the bow, taking time to explore the easily accessible open holds. Stripped of cargo, they now shelter soldierfish, lionfish, gobies and hawkfish. At the bow look for turtles, groupers and large schools of fusiliers and jacks.

From here double back toward the stern, following the ship's rail along the outer hull. Embellished with encrusting sponges and coral growth, the hull is crawling with little creatures such as pipefish, shrimp and nudibranchs. Near the stern you'll find the crew quarters and wheelhouse, where colorful patches of tubastrea and other encrusting organisms now grow in place of the navigation instruments. Reserve plenty of air for your ascent and plan a safety stop atop the mainmast.

Corals and sponges coat the hull and machinery.

15 Hans Hass Place

Named after legendary Austrian underwater explorer Hans Hass, this protected marine area is an excellent site for divers of all skill levels as well as macrophotographers. On the south side of Gulhi Falhu a 100m stretch of the reef has broken off, leaving an indentation that offers protection from currents. Facing Vaadhoo Kandu, the site is carved with overhangs and rock formations starting as shallow as 5m down to about 30m. The ceilings

Location: South side of Gulhi Falhu

Depth Range: 5-30m (16-100ft)

Access: Boat or live-aboard

Expertise Rating: Novice

in many of the overhangs flaunt small purple sea fans with pretty lace patterns.

You'll find a host of marine life within the formations, including soldierfish, tiny shrimp and gobies, arrowhead soapfish, broom filefish, marbled groupers and coral hinds. The reef is also home to an abundance of magnificent anemones, most of which boast brilliantly hued undersides. Turtles, octopuses, and honeycomb and blackcheek morays are also common here.

While suffering some damage from the 1998 El Niño, the shallow reeftop is slowly recovering and still supports myriad butterflyfish and large schools of convict and powder-blue surgeonfish. Observant divers may also spot the well-disguised leaf scorpionfish and red-cheeked pipefish.

A Maldives anemonefish nestles into its host.

16 Lion's Head

The starting point of this dive is a large rock formation, loosely resembling a lion's head, that protrudes into current-swept Vaadhoo Kandu. Before the area was declared a protected marine area, sharks were fed here on a regular basis. Though feeding is now discouraged, plenty of sharks still patrol the reef.

Depending on the current, you can follow the wall in either direction, but the

Location: West of Thila Fushi

Depth Range: 3-35m (10-115ft)

Access: Boat or live-aboard

Expertise Rating: Intermediate

east side holds more interest. At 5m and between 20 and 25m you'll find a series of overhangs and caves filled with soldier-fish, lobsters and groupers. The wall itself is festooned with branching and encrusting sponges in colors ranging from red and orange to violet. Sea fans, crinoids and an abundance of anemones and corals further enhance the reef. Grey reef sharks often cruise the wall at 20m and below, and hawksbill turtles frequent the shallows.

Schooling batfish, surgeonfish and clouds of anthias are especially active when the current is ripping, while keen observers will also spot camouflaged creatures such as octopuses, pipefish and venomous stonefish and leaf scorpionfish. Though currents here are sometimes strong, there are plenty of overhangs in which to seek shelter, at least temporarily. The shallow reeftop at 3 to 5m is ideal for your safety stop as well as for snorkelers.

Currents sweep the exposed reef at Lion's Head, supporting abundant marine life.

17 Hembadhoo Wreck

This excellent dive is a short swim from the Hembadhoo jetty. Sunk as an artificial reef in 1988, this former cargo ship is about 16m long and sits upright on the seafloor at 22m, topping out at 15m.

Over the years the wreck has developed its own ecosystem and now offers an abundance of marine life and colorful photo opportunities. The ship is blanketed in soft-coral trees, black coral trees and multicolored sponges. Friendly Napoleonfish are likely to greet you, and you'll spot a variety of morays, which may peer back at you from a porthole. Dense clouds of glass-

Location: South of Hembadhoo

Depth Range: 15-22m (50-72ft)

Access: Boat or shore

Expertise Rating: Novice

fish inhabit the cabin, while nudibranchs and flatworms slowly negotiate the encrusted hull. Keep an eye out for juvenile boxfish, wrasses and emperor angelfish, as well as schools of rabbitfish and the occasional eagle ray.

South Male' Atoll (Kaafu) Dive Sites

MICHAEL AW

Maafushi tuna fishermen sell their catch in Male'.

South Male' was among the first atolls to open to tourism and now boasts more than a dozen resorts, many in business since the 1970s. Most of the resort islands are in the southern half of the atoll, with good access to prime dive sites. Eleven islands are entirely uninhabited.

The population numbers less than 1,500, with only three locally inhabited islands, each with its own personality and economic link to nearby Male'. Gulhi is home to a privately owned shipyard, while anglers from the traditional fishing village Maafushi, the capital of the atoll, catch tuna to sell at market in Male'. Guraidhoo is the largest island and offers safe overnight anchorage for safari dive vessels.

South Male' Atoll (Kaafu) Dive Sites	Good Snorkeling	Novice	Intermediate	Advanced
18 Vaadhoo Caves	●			●
19 Embudhoo Canyon	●		●	
20 Embudhoo Kandu			●	
21 Kuda Giri		●		
22 Cocoa Corner	●			●
23 Kandooma Caves				●
24 Medhu Faru	●		●	
25 Guraidhoo Corner	●			●
26 Vaagali Bodu Thila			●	

Traditionally, the island was known for boatbuilding and maintenance, but now souvenir shops line the main street. At the heart of the resort islands and equipped with a helicopter pad for tourist transfers, Guraidhoo is visited daily by tourists from around the world.

Diving in South Male' is possible year-round, though conditions and visibility are generally best during the northeast monsoon season. Kandu diving is the big draw. Massive volumes of water flush through only six narrow channels along the eastern reef wall, creating very strong currents and thrilling dive experiences.

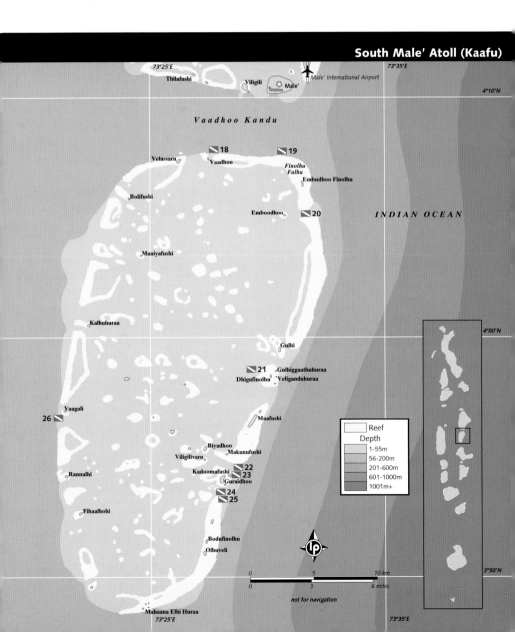

18 Vaadhoo Caves

The reef directly north of Vaadhoo drops vertically into Vaadhoo Kandu, the wide, deep channel separating North and South

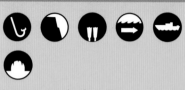

Location: North of Vaadhoo

Depth Range: 3-40m+ (10-130ft+)

Access: Boat or live-aboard

Expertise Rating: Advanced

Soft corals tint one large overhang bright blue.

Male' Atolls. This current-flushed drop-off is punctuated with overhangs and a series of large caves filled with marine life.

While the reef rises as shallow as 3m, the cave formations start at 7m, with some as deep as 40m. To the west a huge overhang between 15 and 30m features a ceiling densely covered in stunning blue soft corals. Most caves are packed with soldierfish and squirrelfish, and some serve as cleaning stations for sleek unicornfish. Look for turtles and stingrays at rest on the sand or rubble cave floors.

When a current is running through Vaadhoo Kandu, the many caves allow you to temporarily duck out of the current and snap photos before drifting to the next cave.

19 Embudhoo Canyon

Embudhoo Canyon is a unique, exciting site offering striking topography. A large section of Finolhu Falhu has broken off from the main reef, leaving a cavity at least 200m long. The resulting channel, or canyon, between the rock and the main reef is about 50m long, 5m wide and 15 to 20m deep.

Start your dive outside the narrow channel, exploring caves at about 30m

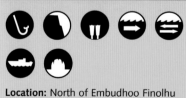

Location: North of Embudhoo Finolhu

Depth Range: 5-30m (16-100ft)

Access: Boat or live-aboard

Expertise Rating: Intermediate

on both the main reef and the ocean side of the large rock. Soldierfish, squirrelfish and the occasional angelfish fill most of the caves. The outer reef is also the best spot to encounter sharks, eagle rays and schooling black snappers. Be wary of strong currents.

The canyon itself is very dramatic and also features a cave worth exploring. If the current allows, slowly circle your way to the top of the rock, checking out the numerous nooks for moray eels and other critters. Expect to be continuously surrounded by schooling fusiliers and trevallies throughout your

dive. Spend your safety stop atop the main reef at 5m.

If startled, morays may bite defensively.

20 | Embudhoo Kandu

A protected marine area, Embudhoo Kandu offers excellent opportunities to observe pelagic fish.

The south side of this wide, relatively shallow channel is known as **Embudhoo Express**, an advanced dive in strong currents. Start this exhilarating 2km drift dive from the southwest corner, often referred to as "Shark Point," and descend to 30m, where the reef meets the atoll wall. This vertical drop into the abyss is the best spot to hang for a while and watch an abundance of grey and white-tip reef sharks patrolling the deep blue.

From here keep the reef to your left and make your way around the corner, often in the company of several sharks, eagle rays or Napoleonfish. Small caves on the corner are home to well-camouflaged brown-marbled groupers and dense schools of soldierfish. Once inside the channel, you can enter a larger cave that reaches from 25m all the way to 5m. Blanketed with colorful sponges, it's home to giant morays, lionfish and beautiful angelfish.

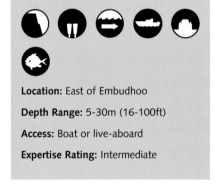

Location: East of Embudhoo

Depth Range: 5-30m (16-100ft)

Access: Boat or live-aboard

Expertise Rating: Intermediate

The north side of the channel features a thila that climbs from 30 to 12m. When currents subside, this is an excellent dive for photographers and less experienced divers. Soft and hard corals wreathe the thila, which is home to lionfish, octopuses, moray eels and a range of colorful tropicals. This site is also a magnet for schooling fusiliers, jacks and black-and-white snappers. Take time to explore a series of caves on the northeast corner of the adjacent main reef, or cut through a narrow canyon that splits the thila and leads out into the channel.

21 Kuda Giri

Sunk as an artificial reef, a steel wreck is the main highlight of this site, though the giri itself has lots to offer. The pinnacle is small enough to be circumnavigated and ranges from 3 to 25m deep. Glassfish, soldierfish, octopuses and brown-marbled groupers hole up in the reef's various nooks and caves. You'll also find nudibranchs, flatworms and shrimp, all excellent macrophotography subjects. On the reeftop, look among the sponge-coated hard corals to spot scorpionfish, hawkfish, tangs and butterflyfish.

The wreck sits upright on her keel at 30m, topping out at 15m. Red, yellow and orange sponges paint the propeller and parts of the hull, as do thriving colonies of tubastrea cup coral. Divers regularly spot lionfish and morays, particularly on the bridge, and the wreck also shelters groupers, hawkfish, shoals of glassfish and many tiny gobies and blennies. Another popular attraction is

Location: West of Dhigufinolhu

Depth Range: 3-30m (10-100ft)

Access: Boat or live-aboard

Expertise Rating: Novice

the huge resident school of batfish that hovers around the wreck. Extremely curious and friendly, the batfish make excellent portrait subjects.

The sand surrounding the wreck is home to garden eels, sand-divers, prawngobies and sandperch. However, the seafloor slopes pretty quickly, so pay attention to your depth.

Because currents are moderate to absent, safari boat operators often use Kuda Giri as a checkout dive. However, anyone who appreciates small critters, calm conditions and plenty of photo ops will be happy diving this site.

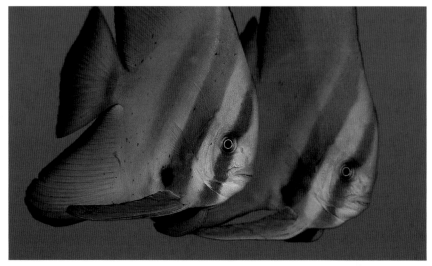

Photographers will find plenty of subjects, such as these approachable, photogenic batfish.

Artificial Reefs

The best way for divers to understand reef evolution is to observe artificial reefs at different stages of development. Artificial reefs can take hold on any submerged foreign object, such as a ship or plane, concrete blocks, tires or a simple bottle. Even disintegrating wrecks lend themselves well to marine life encrustation and offer shelter to many species.

How well life takes to an artificial reef depends on three main factors:

Location Artificial reefs placed in open, sandy areas become an oasis for surrounding marine life and attract denser growth than objects placed onto an existing reef. The shelter they provide at current-swept sites often attracts species otherwise rarely seen. Juveniles commonly seek refuge here, while hydroids and encrusting sponges draw an abundant nudibranch population.

Material Steel provides an excellent growing surface for coral. While rubber and aluminum objects may provide good shelter, they typically don't support coral growth.

Age The longer an object is underwater, the more life it attracts. Many corals take years to establish themselves, while other species start growing within a few months after the object has been submerged.

22 Cocoa Corner

This site is best dived during an incoming current, starting on the ocean side of the Cocoa Beach resort house reef and drifting into the channel. The channel is quite deep, dropping to 40m, but the reeftop reaches within 5m of the surface, so you can pick your depth.

As you drift toward the corner, keep your eyes peeled for cruising grey and whitetip reef sharks and eagle rays. If the current allows, swim into the channel to a coral outcrop at about 30m that seems very popular with whitetips and turtles.

Location: South of Makunufushi

Depth Range: 5-40m (16-130ft)

Access: Boat or live-aboard

Expertise Rating: Advanced

Work your way back to the channel wall. Near the corner, between 5 and 20m, you'll find lots of caves and undercuts, some very large. Black coral trees, whip corals and sea fans all thrive along the current-swept wall. In strong currents the caves offer a chance to pause and watch schooling jacks and fusiliers. In the caves themselves you'll find soldierfish and squirrelfish, as well as hawksbill turtles, stingrays, unicornfish and snappers. The shallow reeftop is home to grazing tangs, butterflyfish and friendly turtles.

23 Kandooma Caves

This site on the northeast corner of the Kandooma Tourist Resort house reef is an extraordinary dive, featuring a number of huge caves that rank among the largest in the Maldives.

Start your dive on the ocean side of the corner, making your way to the bottom to watch the grey reef sharks and

Location: East of Kandoomafushi

Depth Range: 5-40m (16-130ft)

Access: Boat or live-aboard

Expertise Rating: Advanced

This network of caves is a natural lair for honeycomb morays.

occasional hammerheads that patrol this area. Be sure to hug the wall as you round the corner, as currents can be ferocious.

Just inside the channel are the two largest caves, the first one boasting a skylight. Both caves are quite dark, so be sure to bring a dive light with you. If you plan any photography, you'll want to rig a spotter light on your camera setup. Bursting with life, the caves are home to brown-marbled groupers, soldierfish, sweetlips, stunning emperor and blue-face angelfish and the occasional resting hawksbill turtle.

Farther inside the channel are more overhangs and caves, some of them quite shallow. Look amid this maze of formations for small schools of batfish, juvenile clown triggerfish, giant, blackcheek and honeycomb morays and many other colorful reef species.

24 Medhu Faru

On the north side of Guraidhoo Kandu (a protected marine area), Medhu Faru's south side is a fantastic dive, particularly when the current flows into the atoll.

Location: North side of Guraidhoo Kandu

Depth Range: 5-35m (16-115ft)

Access: Boat or live-aboard

Expertise Rating: Intermediate

Start on the outside wall, which slopes to a ledge at 30m before plunging into the deep. As you slowly work your way around the corner into the channel, you'll find beautiful sea fans and whip corals, schooling longfin and masked bannerfish, turtles and moray eels.

Just off the reef near the corner is a large rock formation entirely blanketed with soft corals of every imaginable color. Oriental sweetlips, phantom bannerfish and collared butterflyfish flock around this rock, while fusiliers and jacks swirl above you in the water column.

As you round the corner, the wall drops off steeply and features numerous overhangs and caves, home to soldierfish, emperor angelfish and unicornfish. You'll likely spot stingrays and prawn-gobies along the sandy channel bottom at 35m.

Keep an eye out for longfin and masked bannerfish, each a species of butterflyfish.

25 Guraidhoo Corner

Perhaps because Guraidhoo Kandu was declared a protected marine area several years ago, this site ranks among the best for fish-watching and photography. Despite strong currents and throngs of divers, this spot is definitely worth a number of dives.

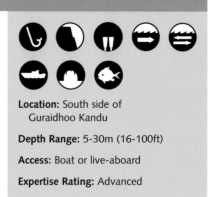

Location: South side of Guraidhoo Kandu

Depth Range: 5-30m (16-100ft)

Access: Boat or live-aboard

Expertise Rating: Advanced

Enter on the ocean side of the channel and you'll probably be greeted by schools of fusiliers, rainbow runners and jacks, or by one of the friendly Napoleonfish. One of them is huge, close to 2m long, with the characteristic hump on its head. The channel bottoms out at 35m, then drops abruptly into the deep. This is the best spot to observe grey reef sharks and other pelagics.

Inside the channel the reef wall is carved with numerous small overhangs and undercuts, as well as one large overhang that reaches from 5 to 30m. This is a good place to shelter from the current and check out the resident marine life. Farther inside the channel you'll find a rock outcrop at 30m with an arch blan-

keted in multihued soft corals. A school of sweetlips and long-jawed squirrelfish is usually willing to pose beneath the arch for photographers. Throughout the dive you're likely to encounter honeycomb morays, large schools of batfish and bannerfish, and several very friendly turtles.

Wind and waves often make the surface choppy at this site, and currents are troublesome at times, with possible whirlpool effects and vertical currents. On your ascent, keep an eye out for passing dive boats.

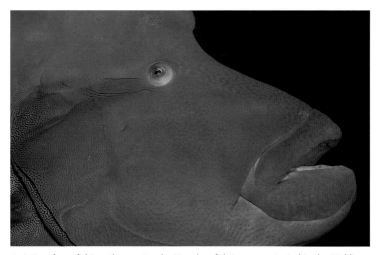

A victim of overfishing, the spectacular Napoleonfish is now protected in the Maldives.

26 Vaagali Bodu Thila

On the west side of the atoll, this large thila is in the middle of a wide channel, just south of uninhabited Vaagali. Shielded from the weather for most of the year, the site is quite exposed during the southwest monsoon season. The sheer west side of the thila faces the open ocean and is an excellent spot to observe pelagics and large schools of fish.

The most spectacular side, however, is the thila's north side. Between 15 and

Location: South of Vaagali

Depth Range: 5-35m (16-115ft)

Access: Boat or live-aboard

Expertise Rating: Intermediate

A coral hind and soldierfish paint the reef red beneath an overhanging bed of bright soft corals.

30m you can explore a number of caves and overhangs filled with life. Sea whips, black coral trees and lush soft-coral trees line the formations, which are home to sweetlips, bluelined snappers and soldierfish. Outside the caves the sloping wall is also graced with multihued soft corals. Throughout your dive you may see friendly turtles and Napoleonfish, as well as swirling schools of bannerfish.

Felidhoo Atoll (Vaavu) Dive Sites

In the middle of the archipelago, boot-shaped Felidhoo Atoll remains relatively undeveloped despite its proximity to Male'. While there are only two resorts, Dhiggiri and Alimathaa, the atoll is frequented by a fleet of safari dive boats that cater to those seeking tranquil beauty and superb diving.

Safari boats flock to Felidhoo.

The atoll comprises about 10 uninhabited islands and five locally inhabited islands. The capital island, Felidhoo, is on the east side, while to the north, picturesque Fulidhoo offers a good harbor and is a popular stopover for safari boats. Locals from both islands are well known for their dance performances. Women perform the "pot dance," or *bandiyaa*, while the *bodu beru*, or "big drum," is popular with the men.

Along the foot of the atoll is Fotteyo Falhu, the longest unbroken reef in the Maldives. It stretches for 55km (34 miles), from Hurahu Kandu in the east to Rakeedhoo Kandu on the atoll's south tip.

Felidhoo Atoll (Vaavu) Dive Sites	Good Snorkeling	Novice	Intermediate	Advanced
27 Dhiggiri Kandu				●
28 Medhu Kandu	●		●	
29 Miyaru Kandu	●		●	
30 Devana Kandu	●		●	
31 Keyodhoo Thila (Cippo Thila)	●	●		
32 Fushi Kandu	●		●	
33 Fotteyo	●		●	
34 Rakeedhoo Kandu	●			●
35 Vattaru Kandu	●			●
36 Anbaraa Thila	●	●		
37 Kudaboli Thila				●

Just west of its namesake kandu, Rakeedhoo is a traditional fishing village, with neat coral stone houses lining the streets. The island offers a good overnight anchorage to safari boats planning to dive Rakeedhoo Kandu early the next morning. A few kilometers south of Rakeedhoo, small, circular Vattaru Falhu is home to one uninhabited island and one popular dive site, Vattaru Kandu.

Kandu drift diving is the norm, with vertical walls that plunge to great depths, making the sites both superb and challenging. During the northeast monsoon season, ocean currents flush the eastern kandus of plankton and cloudy lagoon water, leaving gin-clear visibility, ideal for observing sharks and other pelagics. At the same time, plankton-rich currents sweep the west side, providing the perfect feeding ground for mantas and whale sharks.

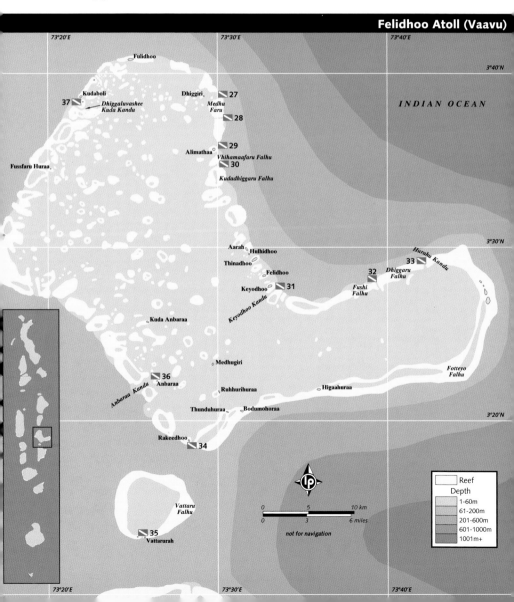

Felidhoo Atoll (Vaavu)

27 Dhiggiri Kandu

Flushed by powerful ocean currents, this channel is well known for pelagic activity. The extreme depth and strong flow definitely make this an advanced dive. It's best approached on an incoming current.

Location: East of Dhiggiri

Depth Range: 20-40m+ (65-130ft+)

Access: Boat or live-aboard

Expertise Rating: Advanced

Enter the water well outside the northeast lip of the channel and descend to the terraced corner at 40m, where all the action happens. If the current allows, swim toward the drop-off, where the wall plunges to great depths. Pelagics you may encounter include grey reef sharks, eagle rays, large schools of barracuda and jacks.

From here keep the wall to your right and drift through the channel, slowly ascending as you go. Blanketed in soft corals, several rocks rise from the sandy channel bottom, but they're still at significant depth, below 25m, so be sure to watch your air supply.

28 Medhu Kandu

This fairly narrow channel is about 250m across. Whitetip reef sharks and

Location: South of Medhu Faru

Depth Range: 5-30m (16-100ft)

Access: Boat or live-aboard

Expertise Rating: Intermediate

You'll find soft corals, sponges and sea squirts.

stingrays rest along the sandy channel bottom to the north, the deep end, while eagle rays and hammerheads frequent the drop-off at the channel mouth. Also near the drop-off are several worthwhile caves, at about 35m.

On the south side of the channel is a large, fairly shallow thila formation. Several coral rocks protrude from the thila's sloping sides, attracting schooling fish such as oriental sweetlips, pennant bannerfish, fusiliers and collared butterflyfish. Photographers with wide-angle setups will especially appreciate the rocks, which boast colorful soft corals, tunicates and sponges. Keep an eye out for hawksbill turtles, octopuses and scorpionfish. This side also offers the best snorkeling.

29 Miyaru Kandu

This narrow passage is best approached on an incoming current. Divers can cross the 100m channel, increasing their odds for pelagic encounters.

Enter the water at least 20m north of the channel entrance, as you'll need enough time to reach the bottom at 30m. You'll quickly find a cave formation filled with long-jawed squirrelfish and soldierfish. There are several more caves along the drop-off, some sheltering black and wire corals.

However, to many divers the main attraction is a resident school of grey reef sharks. *Miyaru* means "shark" in Dhivehi, and you almost always spot these predators on either or both sides of the channel. You may also see eagle rays, barracuda and jacks. Hammerhead sharks gather here in the early morning.

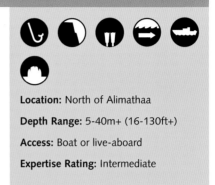

Location: North of Alimathaa

Depth Range: 5-40m+ (16-130ft+)

Access: Boat or live-aboard

Expertise Rating: Intermediate

If the current allows, cross the channel to the south tip and meander through a garden of soft corals and large gorgonian sea fans. From here drift into the channel and ascend into the shallows, where you'll find whitetip and blacktip reef sharks, turtles and schooling bannerfish.

Divers and photographers are thrilled by the fast moves of the resident grey reef sharks.

30 Devana Kandu

A long, narrow thila divides Devana Kandu into two narrow passages. Divers commonly spot eagle rays and grey reef sharks at the channel ends, particularly during the northeast monsoon season, when currents flow into the atoll. The entire channel is a protected marine area.

Location: Between Vihamaafaru Falhu and Kudadhiggaru Falhu

Depth Range: 5-30m (16-100ft)

Access: Boat or live-aboard

Expertise Rating: Intermediate

An eagle ray's "wingspan" can exceed 2m.

The south passage is perhaps the more scenic dive, boasting several small pinnacles blanketed in soft corals. These pinnacles are fish magnets and, therefore, are equally attractive to photographers. You're likely to see large morays, several species of butterflyfish and other tropicals such as blue-face and emperor angelfish.

31 Keyodhoo Thila (Cippo Thila)

This spectacular thila is relatively small, making it easy to circumnavigate in one dive. Although inside Keyodhoo Kandu, it's somewhat shielded from currents by the shape of the channel wall. Operators usually tie the boat to the thila and use the mooring line for descents and ascents.

Location: Keyodhoo Kandu

Depth Range: 3-25m (10-82ft)

Access: Boat or live-aboard

Expertise Rating: Novice

On the south side of the thila is a large crack where thousands of anthias gather among orange-hued soft corals. The west side sports a spectacular array of sea fans and black coral trees, some sheltering longnose hawkfish. Coral hinds and moray eels frequent cleaning stations among the nooks that lace the thila, and throughout your dive you'll also see stunning clusters of soft corals, sea whips, tunicates and sponges. Amid this profusion of color you'll find tropicals such as schooling collared butterflyfish, batfish, bannerfish, long-jawed squirrelfish and oriental sweetlips.

A large number of magnificent anemones make their home atop the thila. At dusk they curl up, revealing their colorful undersides.

A Clean Break

Symbiosis occurs throughout the marine world—associations in which two dissimilar organisms share a mutually beneficial relationship. One of the most interesting of these relationships is found at cleaning stations, where one animal (the symbiont) advertises its grooming services to potential clients with inviting, undulating movements. Often this is done near a coral head or, particularly in the Maldives, beneath an overhang.

Various species of cleaners such as wrasses and shrimp care for customers of all sizes and species. Larger fish such as sharks and mantas generally frequent cleaning stations serviced by angelfish, butterflyfish and larger wrasses, while turtles often seek out herbivorous tangs eager to rid the turtles of their algae buildup.

Customers hover in line, waiting their turn. When the cleaner attends to a customer—perhaps a grouper, parrotfish or even moray eel—they often enter the customer's mouth to perform dental hygiene and may even exit through the fish's gills. Although the customer could have an easy snack, it would never attempt to swallow the essential cleaner. The large fish benefit from the removal of parasites and dead tissue, while the cleaners are provided with a meal.

If you carefully approach a cleaning station, you'll get closer to many fish than is normally possible and observe interesting behavior not seen anywhere else on the reef.

32 Fushi Kandu

Two dive profiles are popular in this narrow channel. You can cross the channel, following the edge of the drop-off to observe pelagics, or you can enter the water on either outside wall and drift around the corner until you come to a narrow thila about 50m inside the channel.

Near the drop-off you'll likely see reef sharks, eagle rays, jacks, tuna and large schools of fusiliers. Inside the channel and on the thila you'll find beautiful coral growth, including black coral trees, sea fans and soft corals. The sandy channel bottom is home to stingrays,

Location: Between Fushi Falhu and Dhiggaru Falhu

Depth Range: 2-35m (7-115ft)

Access: Boat or live-aboard

Expertise Rating: Intermediate

decorated gobies, and prawn-gobies with symbiotic blind shrimp.

The thila tops out around 10m, while the channel reeftop is only 2m deep, ideal for snorkeling. While the shallow hard-coral garden is still recovering from coral bleaching damage, you will encounter clouds of grazing butterflyfish and tangs, parrotfish and many types of wrasses.

Common throughout the Maldives, blotched fantail rays sift the sand for mollusks and crustaceans.

33 Fotteyo

Considered one of the prime sites in the Maldives, Fotteyo is indeed an extraordinary dive. Although there are several options to explore this huge site, it's usually best to enter the water on the outside of Dhiggaru Falhu, the reef west of the channel. Near the corner is a gorgeous cave at 30m and another one at about 40m, both hosting whip corals, black corals, sea fans and clouds of fish.

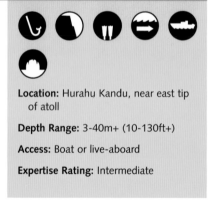

Location: Hurahu Kandu, near east tip of atoll

Depth Range: 3-40m+ (10-130ft+)

Access: Boat or live-aboard

Expertise Rating: Intermediate

As you continue around the bend, you'll come to several caves, huge overhangs and arches, all festooned with pale soft corals that densely blanket the entrances, ceilings and walls. Resembling blooming cherry trees in the spring, the caves are known as "Cherry Caves." The depth here varies, with the more interesting formations between 25 and 35m.

The 200m-wide channel is divided by a large thila, essentially splitting the channel in two for the first 150m. One option, especially on an incoming current, is to enter the channel immediately and swim to a large sandy patch at about 25m. Here you'll find resting whitetips, as well as prawn-gobies and their accompanying snapping shrimp. If the current continues to push you along, stay on the west side and slowly head up into the shallows. You're likely to see turtles, octopuses and myriad butterflyfish and tangs.

Other options include finishing your dive at 5m atop the thila or entering the channel on the east side of the thila. On this side you'll probably meet the resident sweetlips or one of the friendly turtles. Just inside the channel is "Trigger Alley," where titan and yellow-margin triggerfish are abundant. Be wary during nesting season, as they can be quite aggressive.

If the current allows you to stay along the vertical drop-off at the mouth of the channel, you may encounter reef sharks, hammerheads and cruising eagle rays. Keep your eyes on the reef wall to spot the rare deepwater Indian butterflyfish.

The pale soft corals that drape the caves and overhangs evoke cherry trees in bloom.

34 Rakeedhoo Kandu

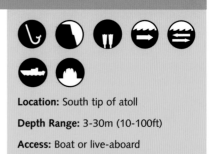

Just east of the fishing island Rakeedhoo, this kandu is regularly swept by strong currents that provide nutrients to abundant coral growth and a wide range of marine life. Both corners of the channel mouth feature magnificent caves and plenty of fish.

Location: South tip of atoll

Depth Range: 3-30m (10-100ft)

Access: Boat or live-aboard

Expertise Rating: Advanced

On the east corner is a vertical wall pitted with several large caves between 20 and 40m. The sand and rubble cave floors are popular resting spots for stingrays and nurse sharks. Napoleonfish, turtles and schooling reef fish frequent the shallows.

Most divers flock to the west or Rakeedhoo side of the channel, as the corner is beautifully terraced between 20 and 50m before the wall abruptly drops. Below each plateau you'll discover caves festooned with blue soft corals that drape from the ceilings. The deeper caves also shelter black corals and large sea fans. Snappers, long-jawed squirrelfish and soldierfish inhabit the caves, while sharks and other pelagics cruise the channel.

Plan your dive carefully and stick to your profile. If you start your dive inside the channel, be ready to deal with turbulence and breakers at the channel mouth. On an incoming flow, the current splits on the east corner, possibly pushing you along the outside wall. This is generally safe, though the better features are inside the channel.

35 Vattaru Kandu

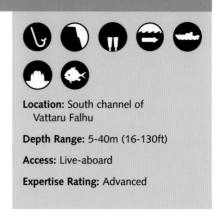

A protected marine area, this 100m-wide kandu is the only break in the circular reef Vattaru Falhu. The best diving is along the east corner and outside wall, just off uninhabited Vattarurah.

Location: South channel of Vattaru Falhu

Depth Range: 5-40m (16-130ft)

Access: Live-aboard

Expertise Rating: Advanced

The corner drops quickly to 40m, then slopes to a sandy seafloor. Reef fish swarm along the wall, while the shallows support legions of anemones. Look amid the sand for sand-divers, garden eels, harems of the exquisite wrasse, and pink-bar prawn-gobies with accompanying snapping shrimp.

At the corner, squirrelfish and soldierfish fill several overhangs between 10 and 20m. Just outside the channel, pinkish-blue and white soft corals decorate part of the sheer wall and a series of caves. Keep an eye on the blue water for manta rays, sharks and turtles, as well as schooling fusiliers, barracuda and jacks.

Depending on the current, you could start from the outside, keeping the wall to your right and finishing inside the channel, or vice versa, keeping the wall to your left. At the channel mouth you may want to visit the middle of the passage to look for sharks, then swim back to the east side.

36 | Anbaraa Thila

Divers can easily circumnavigate this small thila north of uninhabited Anbaraa. The thila sits just inside Anbaraa Kandu, which supplies plenty of nutrients to support ample marine life. Generally calm conditions make it an ideal site for novices, night divers and macrophotographers.

Location: Inside atoll, north of Anbaraa

Depth Range: 5-27m (16-90ft)

Access: Boat or live-aboard

Expertise Rating: Novice

Anemonefish secrete a mucus that neutralizes their hosts' stinging cells—reason enough to gloat.

Throughout your dive you'll see lots of anemones, bubble corals, hard corals and black corals. The fish are extremely friendly here, and it's easy to get good close-up photographs of blue-face and emperor angelfish, saddleback coralgroupers and even octopuses. Peer into the reef crevices to find crimson soldierfish and clouds of silvery glassfish.

The shallow hard-coral garden is slowly recovering from coral bleaching, though it still provides a home to myriad butterflyfish, parrotfish and tangs, as well as venomous scorpionfish.

Adult blue-face angelfish are often solitary swimmers.

37 Kudaboli Thila

This colorful, 50m-long thila is in the middle of the channel. To enjoy the coral bloom to its fullest, begin your dive on an outgoing current. As the area of greatest interest is relatively small, you should enter the water at least 50m east of the thila, then drift down to the right spot.

Location: Dhiggaluvashee Kuda Kandu

Depth Range: 5-30m (16-100ft)

Access: Boat or live-aboard

Expertise Rating: Advanced

The highlight here is a huge slab of rock that has broken away from the thila and now lies parallel to it. This slice is covered in orange soft corals, ranging from bright orange to subtle pastel hues. You'll also spot clusters of tubastrea cup corals, as well as a few black coral trees. Multicolored soft corals also blanket several overhangs and windows, which are especially photogenic from either the north or south side. Coral hinds, squirrelfish and swirling anthias frequent the overhangs. In the channel just below the slab, at about 30m, you'll find more formations boasting beautiful soft corals, yellow being the dominant hue. Look for schooling long-jawed squirrelfish and sweetlips.

Between the rock slab and the thila is a cut lined with scattered coral heads. Look along its rubble floor for stingrays, octopuses and a resident school of bannerfish. The top of the thila is home to more octopuses, turtles and schools of tangs, sweetlips and butterflyfish.

In a strong current, be very careful upon surfacing. The channel opening lies exposed to prevailing southwest winds, and currents can stir up big eddies and breakers.

Kudaboli Thila is laced with interesting swim-throughs, each boasting a splash of colorful soft corals.

Mulaku Atoll (Meemu)
Dive Sites

Mulaku is 47km (29 miles) long and 30km (19 miles) wide. Its 5,000 residents inhabit nine fishing islands along the east side of the atoll. Only two of the atoll's 35 islands have been developed into tourist resorts—the rest are uninhabited. This is a popular port of call for vessels plying between the southern atolls and Male'. While the main occupation is fishing, agriculture is also performed on a much smaller scale, with successful yam farms on Kolhuvaariyaafushi and Boli Mulah. Mulaku remains largely unexplored by divers, since the atoll was only opened to tourism in 1999. Safari boats and the two resident dive resorts have only begun to explore the reefs.

Mulaku offers long stretches of barrier reef, interrupted by five deep, narrow channels along the northern reef and one wide channel on the east side. The west side features shorter stretches of reef, cut with narrow channels that are best explored during the southwest monsoon season. The inside of the atoll is studded with innumerable thila and giri formations.

Only recently opened to tourism, Mulaku remains largely unexplored.

Mulaku Atoll (Meemu) Dive Sites

		Good Snorkeling	Novice	Intermediate	Advanced
38	**Mulaku Kandu**			●	
39	**Easy Express**				●
40	**Shark's Tongue**			●	
41	**Giant Clam**	●	●		

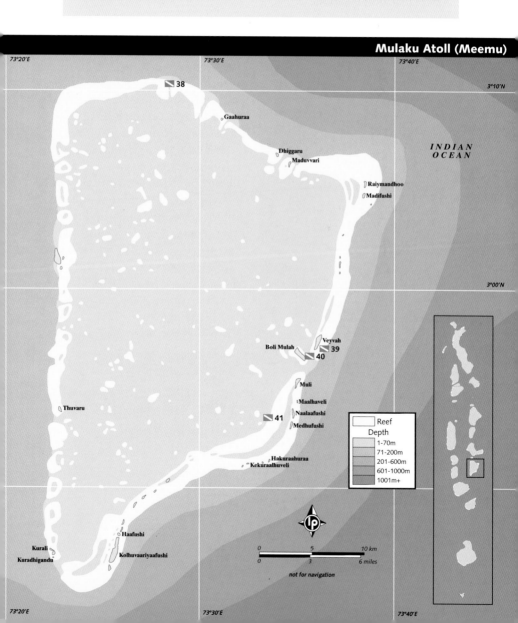

Mulaku Atoll (Meemu)

73°20'E   73°30'E   73°40'E

3°10'N

INDIAN
OCEAN

38

Gaahuraa

Dhiggaru
Maduvvari

Raiymandhoo
Madifushi

3°00'N

Veyvah
Boli Mulah   39
40

Muli

Thuvaru

Maalhaveli
Naalaafushi
41   Medhufushi

Hakuraahuraa
Kekuraalhuveli

	Reef
	Depth
	1-70m
	71-200m
	201-600m
	601-1000m
	1001m+

Haafushi

Kurali
Kuradhigandu   Kolhuvaariyaafushi

0   5   10 km
0   3   6 miles

not for navigation

73°20'E   73°30'E   73°40'E

38 Mulaku Kandu

Divers at this fantastic site usually drop in along the outside wall of the barrier reef. Once you reach the corner, the reef wall drops in several large steps, each featuring huge overhangs with ceilings covered in pastel blue soft corals.

From here you can swim to the coral pinnacle that sits just off the corner, a

Location: North tip of atoll

Depth Range: 5-35m (16ft-115ft)

Access: Live-aboard

Expertise Rating: Intermediate

Explore a pinnacle thickly cloaked in soft corals.

highlight of the dive. About 10m in diameter, this chimney-like coral formation reaches from 35 to 20m. The entire pinnacle is alive with fish and overgrown with soft corals in every imaginable color. Take time to explore its many windows and overhangs.

Preferably this dive is done on a mild incoming current, so after fully exploring the pinnacle, you can slowly drift into the channel. Once you enter, you'll come across a group of coral rocks at 15m, home to tight schools of long-jawed squirrelfish and oriental sweetlips. The coral rocks are carved with overhangs filled with clouds of glassfish and schools of twinspot and bluelined snappers. To complete your dive, make your way back to the channel wall and ascend.

39 Easy Express

This site comprises the steep outer reef wall east of Veyvah. Depending on the strength and direction of the currents, divers head either north or south.

Boasting a number of coral formations, the reeftop averages about 12m. Here you'll see countless anemones, coral hinds, slender and peacock groupers and a colorful blend of parrotfish, butterflyfish and tangs. Friendly turtles also frequent the shallows.

Location: East of Veyvah

Depth Range: 12-30m (40-100ft)

Access: Boat or live-aboard

Expertise Rating: Advanced

Farther down the steep drop-off, between 12 and 30m, you'll find several

overhangs and caves that shelter giant morays and large marbled groupers. You may also encounter one of the large Napoleonfish. While drifting along this sheer wall, be sure to frequently glance into the blue water to see patrolling sharks, eagle rays and schools of trevallies.

Big marbled groupers lay low in the caves and overhangs.

Watching Sharks

Often portrayed as bloodthirsty, evil killers, most shark species are actually quite shy. Aggression toward humans is rare, and unprovoked attacks on divers are almost unheard of. In fact, sharks face a much greater threat from humans, as people routinely kill sharks for profit and pleasure. For the majority of divers, shark encounters are a highlight.

The Maldives is a great place to observe sharks. These magnificent predators frequent the steep walls just outside atoll channels, where nutrient-rich currents trigger the food chain. Maldivian waters are home to several shark species, including whale sharks, tiger sharks, variegated and silky sharks. Following are descriptions of some of the most commonly observed species:

Grey Reef Shark Often found prowling in or just outside the channels, this fairly stocky species grows to about 1.5m (5ft). Its upper body is gray, while its undersides are pale-gray to white. Other distinguishing features include a white edge on its dorsal fin and black edges on its pelvic and tail fins.

Whitetip Reef Shark Divers spot whitetips either cruising the reef or resting on the sand, often in caves (see photo). It's a smallish shark, with a maximum length of 1.3m (4ft). It sports a long thin body and white tips on the first dorsal fin and upper tip of the tail fin.

Blacktip Reef Shark Though less common than grey and whitetip reef sharks, blacktips often roam among them. Growing up to 1.3m (4ft), this shark is pale brown, with distinct black markings on all fins, particularly visible on the tip of its dorsal fin.

Nurse Shark This very docile bottom-dwelling species rests on the sand in caves and beneath overhangs. Divers often spot just its tail, as the shark generally rests facing into a cave. It can exceed 3m (10ft), but most are between 1.5 and 2m (5 and 7ft). This shark's first dorsal fin is set well back on its body, with a noticeably long tail fin.

40 Shark's Tongue

One of the highlights of this kandu dive is a large, triangular plateau that extends from the east channel wall at about 12m. From there the wall slopes gently to 30m, then drops to the channel floor below 50m. In strong currents this exposed site is an advanced dive.

Location: East of Boli Mulah

Depth Range: 8-25m (26-82ft)

Access: Boat or live-aboard

Expertise Rating: Intermediate

You'll likely spot sleeping whitetip sharks atop the sandy plateau, and both whitetip and grey reef sharks frequent cleaning stations among several coral blocks at 20m. Between 20 and 30m you can also explore a number of worthwhile overhangs. When a current is running, cruising blacktip, grey and silvertip sharks make an appearance.

The reeftop ranges between 8 and 10m and features numerous coral formations frequented by big schools of surgeonfish, fusiliers and snappers. Groups of oriental sweetlips tuck behind the corals, and with a little luck you may encounter one of the resident turtles.

41 Giant Clam

This outstanding site is suitable for divers of all skill levels, as well as snorkelers. Inside the atoll, two small giris rise to within 5m of the surface. Protected from strong currents and large swells, several enormous and beautiful giant clams thrive on the easternmost giri between 8 and 15m.

Location: West of Medhufushi

Depth Range: 5-30m (16-100ft)

Access: Boat or live-aboard

Expertise Rating: Novice

A tridacna giant clam extends its mantle to gather food.

The giris offer equally nice overhangs and small caves between 10 and 30m. Look within the caves for coral hinds, marbled groupers, lobsters and clouds of glassfish. You'll also find juveniles of several species, including leopard wrasses, clown triggerfish, puffers and boxfish. Scattered hard-coral rocks harbor such masters of camouflage as stonefish and scorpionfish, as well as magnificent anemones and colorful schools of butterflyfish, tangs and spotted groupers.

Addu Atoll (Seenu)
Dive Sites

The southernmost atoll of the Maldives archipelago, heart-shaped Addu lies just below the equator. With a diameter of only 18km (11 miles), the atoll comprises long stretches of barrier reef, interrupted by just four channels. A great part of the barrier reef breaks the surface as lush, coconut-rimmed islands. Twenty of these are classified as uninhabited, including one resort, and seven are locally inhabited, with a population of more than 17,000. Made independent by their isolation, islanders even speak differently than other Maldivians.

This is the economic and administrative center of the southern Maldives. The atoll's capital, Hithadhoo, boasts a population of 10,000 and rivals Male' in size and importance. Britain has wielded the biggest influence here in modern history. It based troops on Gan during WWII and added a Royal Air Force field in 1956. The British later built a series of coral causeways to connect the four main islands, providing hundreds of jobs, though marring the environment. When they pulled out in 1976, the British left an airport, several industrial buildings and hundreds of unemployed people who spoke proper English and had experience working for Westerners. When the tourism industry took off in the '70s, many of those formerly employed by the British landed jobs at resorts throughout the Maldives.

Among divers Addu is known for encounters with big fish, including manta rays, sharks, turtles and pelagics. Another highlight is the wreck of the *British Loyalty*, an oil tanker that was torpedoed by the Japanese and later scuttled.

JAMES LYON

As remote as Addu is, every island now has a telephone.

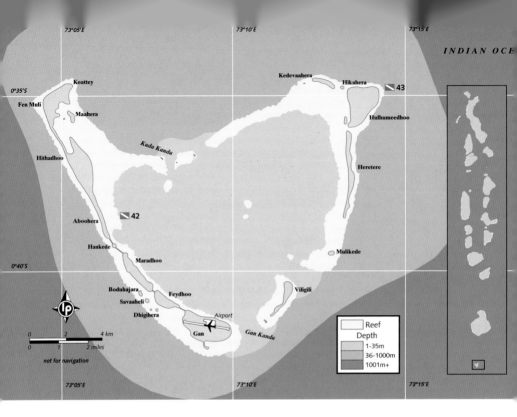

Addu Atoll (Seenu) Dive Sites

	Good Snorkeling	Novice	Intermediate	Advanced
42 British Loyalty			●	
43 Shark Point (Meedhoo Beyra Miyaru)			●	

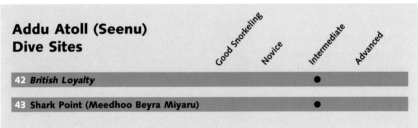

42 *British Loyalty*

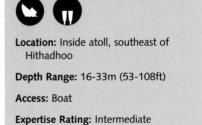

While in service for the British during WWII, this 5,583-ton oil tanker was torpedoed in 1944 by a Japanese submarine, which fired through an opening in the antisubmarine nets at the mouth of Gan Kandu. Disabled but not sunk, the ship remained in the atoll until 1946, when she was towed to her present location and used for target practice till she finally went under.

The 140m wreck now rests on her starboard side in 33m, the port side rising

Location: Inside atoll, southeast of Hithadhoo

Depth Range: 16-33m (53-108ft)

Access: Boat

Expertise Rating: Intermediate

to within 16m of the surface. Hard and soft corals have taken hold throughout

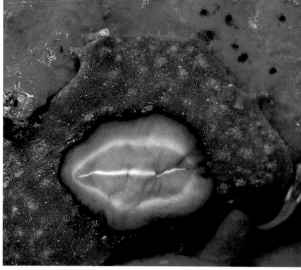

the wreck, while large black corals adorn the propeller at 28m. The hull bears large holes likely caused by the torpedoes, and properly trained divers may enter the wreck.

The site is frequented by turtles, bluefin trevallies and reef fish, and it holds many delights for macrophotographers, including colorful flatworms and nudibranchs, gobies, hawkfish and cardinalfish.

This flatworm's pattern brings to mind a bold neon kiss.

43 Shark Point (Meedhoo Beyra Miyaru)

Off the northeast tip of Hulhumeedhoo the reef drops steeply from 5m to a large sandy plateau at 30m. This area is often referred to as the "Shark Hotel," as divers regularly find whitetip reef sharks at rest on the vast sand terrace, while grey reef sharks cruise the waters overhead.

On the ocean side of the plateau the reef continues to drop to at least 60m. On days with clear visibility, divers can peer into the deep to spot large oceanic sharks. The area lies quite exposed to wind and

Location: Outside atoll, northeast of Hulhumeedhoo

Depth Range: 5-30m (16-100ft)

Access: Boat

Expertise Rating: Intermediate

ocean swells, so exercise proper caution both above and below the surface.

EDWARD SNIJDERS

Small reef fish comprise the bulk of a grey reef shark's diet.

South & North Nilandhoo Atolls (Dhaalu & Faafu) Dive Sites

Newly opened to tourism, these neighboring atolls feature several long barrier reefs, as well as fringing reefs split by many channels. Thilas are common, both at the channel mouths and inside the atolls, and divers will also find scattered reef patches and giris inside the atolls. Besides the interesting underwater topography, the atolls offer pristine topside landscapes and an archaeologically significant history.

The larger of the two atolls, South Nilandhoo is 23km (14 miles) wide and 38km (24 miles) long. A local population of 4,000 inhabits eight of the atoll's 46 islands, while only two have been designated as resort islands.

There are two shipwrecks off Kudahuvadhoo, at the southern tip of the atoll: the *Liffey*, which ran aground in 1879, and the *Utheemu I*, which went down in

MICHAEL AW

Filitheyo is the first resort island to open for business in North Nilandhoo.

South & North Nilandhoo Atolls (Dhaalu & Faafu) Dive Sites	Good Snorkeling	Novice	Intermediate	Advanced
44 Fushi Kandu				●
45 Macro Spot	●	●		
46 Road to Paradise			●	
47 Filitheyo Reef			●	
48 Dolphin's Corner	●		●	
49 Two Brothers	●		●	

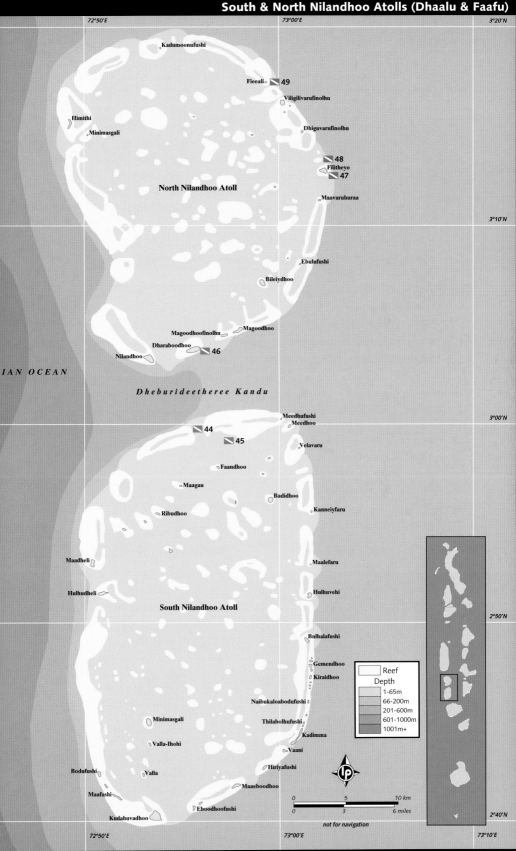

72°50'E — 73°00'E — 3°20'N

Kadumoonufushi

Fieeali 49

Viligilivarufinolhu

Himithi
Minimasgali

Dhiguvarufinolhu

48
Filitheyo
47

North Nilandhoo Atoll

Maavaruhuraa

3°10'N

Ebulufushi

Bileiydhoo

Magoodhoofinolhu   Magoodhoo

Dharaboodhoo
Nilandhoo   46

IAN OCEAN

Dheburideetheree Kandu

3°00'N

Meedhufushi
Meedhoo

44   45

Velavaru

Faandhoo

Maagau
Badidhoo

Ribudhoo   Kanneiyfaru

Maadheli   Maalefaru

Hulhudheli   Hulhuvehi

South Nilandhoo Atoll   2°50'N

Bulhalafushi

Gemendhoo
Kiraidhoo

Naibukaloabodufushi

Thilabolhufushi
Kadimma

Minimasgali

Valla-Ihohi   Vaani

Bodufushi   Hiriyafushi

Valla   Maaeboodhoo

Maafushi
Eboodhoofushi

Kudahuvadhoo

72°50'E   73°00'E   73°10'E
2°40'N

Reef		
Depth		
1-65m		
66-200m		
201-600m		
601-1000m		
1001m+		

0   5   10 km
0   3   6 miles

not for navigation

1960. But as the resorts lie far to the north, dive operators do not visit the wrecks (it would require a dhoni transfer of several hours). As more resorts move into the atoll, further exploration may be possible.

The capital island, Kudahuvadhoo features a mysterious archaeological mound and an old mosque boasting some of the finest masonry in the world, while uninhabited Maadheli is home to ruins of an ancient mosque and settlement. The atoll is also known for its talented traditional goldsmiths and silversmiths.

North Nilandhoo is 27km (17 miles) wide and 30km (19 miles) long, with a population of more than 2,000. Of its 23 islands, five are locally inhabited, while only one of the uninhabited islands, Filitheyo, has been developed into a tourist resort. Since the atoll opened to tourism in December 2000, dive operator Werner Lau and his team of instructors have found a number of exciting and virtually untouched dive sites.

The atoll has a long, rich history. Thor Heyerdahl discovered that Nilandhoo island was a center of Hinduism before the conversion to Islam, once sporting as many as seven temples. Today the island is home to the ancient mosque commissioned by Sultan Mohammed Ibn Abdullah more than 800 years ago, built from the stones of those Hindu temples.

44 Fushi Kandu

Recently designated as a protected marine area, Fushi Kandu is a stunning channel dive on the north end of South Nilandhoo. The channel's west side features a sheer wall that drops from 3m to the seafloor at 30m, while the east corner steps down from 3, 15 and 25m.

Location: South Nilandhoo, north end of atoll

Depth Range: 3-30m (10-100ft)

Access: Boat or live-aboard

Expertise Rating: Advanced

Beware—yellowmouth morays have toxic mucus.

This corner is a great spot to watch eagle rays, whitetip reef sharks and other cruising pelagics.

Inside the channel, several elongated thilas run north to south, dropping from about 10 to 20m. The thilas are covered with hard and soft corals and are frequented by turtles, Napoleonfish and schooling snappers. You'll also find yellowmouth morays, sweetlips, colorful butterflyfish and sedentary species such as scorpionfish.

45 Macro Spot

Protected from currents and swells, this is an easy, shallow site, suitable for snorkelers, novice divers, night divers and those who enjoy macrophotography and diverse marine life.

A large, round giri acts as a nursery for juvenile triggerfish, boxfish, butterflyfish, wrasses and many other species. Numerous overhangs and nooks shelter mantis shrimp, lobsters, cowries, dense clouds of glassfish and various blennies and gobies. You'll also spot popular macro subjects

Location: South Nilandhoo, inside atoll, SE of Fushi Kandu

Depth Range: 3-20m (10-65ft)

Access: Boat or live-aboard

Expertise Rating: Novice

such as stonefish, pipefish, lionfish and frogfish. Keep an eye out for octopuses.

Like a praying mantis, the mantis shrimp uses folded forelimbs to seize prey such as prawns and fish.

46 Road to Paradise

Essentially, this is the Dharaboodhoo house reef. Best dived on an incoming southeast current, it's a thrilling kandu drift dive that promises lots of action and color.

Start on the outside corner and drift into the wide channel, keeping the wall to your left. Eagle rays and huge schools of jacks, perch and groupers patrol the channel mouth. Just inside are numerous

Location: North Nilandhoo, between Magoodhoofinolhu and Dharaboodhoo

Depth Range: 2-33m (7-108ft)

Access: Boat or live-aboard

Expertise Rating: Intermediate

coral formations that rise from the sea-floor at 30m. These formations are blanketed in a sea of swaying soft corals in hues of yellow, blue and red. Schooling butterflyfish and snappers frequent the formations. Look atop the surrounding sand to spot resting stingrays and whitetip sharks.

Once you've checked out these pinnacles, make your way back toward the sheer reef wall, which drops from 2 to 33m. Along this majestic drop-off are several caves stunningly decorated with blue soft corals, tubastrea and sponges. Residents include colorful schools of fusiliers, snappers and soldierfish.

Stingrays inhale through vents behind their eyes.

47 Filitheyo Reef

On the southeast corner of Filitheyo resort island, just outside the channel, this site is actually Filitheyo's house reef, but due to the distance from shore and potentially strong currents, it's only accessible by boat. A protected marine area, the reef literally swirls with thousands of fish, especially when a current is running.

Location: North Nilandhoo, SE of Filitheyo

Depth Range: 2-30m (7-100ft)

Access: Boat or live-aboard

Expertise Rating: Intermediate

Divers are quickly engulfed in clouds of swirling reef fish.

The reef slope drops gradually from the channel corner to the seafloor at 30m. Large steps at 10, 20 and 25m feature several overhangs that are packed with fish. Dense clouds of reef fish also rise into the water column, attracting all types of pelagics, including sharks, rays and trevallies.

Cruising along the bottom of the slope are resident Napoleonfish, an enormous school of batfish and several grey reef sharks.

48 | Dolphin's Corner

In the channel north of Filitheyo, Dolphin's Corner encompasses a sloping plateau between 5 and 33m that extends northward from the channel wall. The site is known as a playground for dolphins. You'll likely see them at the surface as your boat approaches the site. They also brush against the sandy seafloor east and west of the plateau in order to scratch off parasites. Don't expect to spot them on every dive, though, as encounters with dolphins are rare, even at this site. If they are absent, don't despair, as there's plenty of marine life to hold your interest.

Atop the plateau, numerous scattered coral formations attract schooling fish and the occasional whitetip shark. Several large coral pinnacles rise from the

Location: North Nilandhoo, north of Filitheyo

Depth Range: 5-33m (16-108ft)

Access: Boat or live-aboard

Expertise Rating: Intermediate

sand east of the plateau, just off the extended reef wall. Between 15 and 25m deep, they are wreathed in beautiful hard corals, soft corals and sponges. Turtles, eagle rays and lots of reef fish frequent the pinnacles, while the sand supports a field of garden eels and several species of shrimp gobies.

Common in tropical seas worldwide, the spotted dolphin is an active, fast-swimming species.

49 Two Brothers

Sitting near the channel entrance east of Fieeali, the Two Brothers are neighboring thilas. You approach the thilas from the outer reef, which allows an easy drift and chances at pelagic encounters.

From the sandy channel floor at 28m, the smaller of the thilas rises to within 12m of the surface, while its big brother to the north tops out at 3m (which technically makes it a giri). Both are generously adorned with soft corals and sponges, offering fantastic wide-angle photo subjects.

But this is also an excellent macro dive. Frogfish, stonefish and pipefish shelter among the growth on both thilas, and the

Location: North Nilandhoo, east of Fieeali

Depth Range: 3-28m (10-92ft)

Access: Boat or live-aboard

Expertise Rating: Intermediate

larger thila is home to an unusual number and variety of nudibranchs. You're also likely to encounter one of the many resident turtles. On the seafloor surrounding the thilas you'll find shrimp gobies, triplefins and flatworms.

Looking more like a sponge or chunk of coral, a frogfish lies in wait for unsuspecting passersby.

Ari Atoll (Alifu) Dive Sites

Ari Atoll encompasses both the North and South Ari administrative zones and includes neighboring Rasdhoo Atoll and the small island of Thoddoo. One of the largest atolls in the Maldives, Ari is 80km (50 miles) long, 30km (19 miles) wide and boasts 46 uninhabited islands, 27 resort islands and 18 locally inhabited islands, with a population of more than 10,000. Islanders once engaged chiefly in turtle catching, coral collecting and fishing, but now most rely on the tourist industry for their income, through either employment at the resorts or handicraft and souvenir sales. Unfortunately, shark catching remains a strong tradition. While local fishermen originally caught sharks to extract oil for the timber of their dhonis, they now supply the Asian market with shark fins.

Unlike Felidhoo and other atolls, Ari has few long stretches of barrier reef. Except for the south side, which is broken by only two channels, the reef is carved with numerous passages. Although a number of dive sites are in the channels, Ari is particularly known for its thila diving inside the atoll. Rich with marine life, the

Resorts offer island-hopping trips to Dhangethi, a traditional Maldivian fishing village.

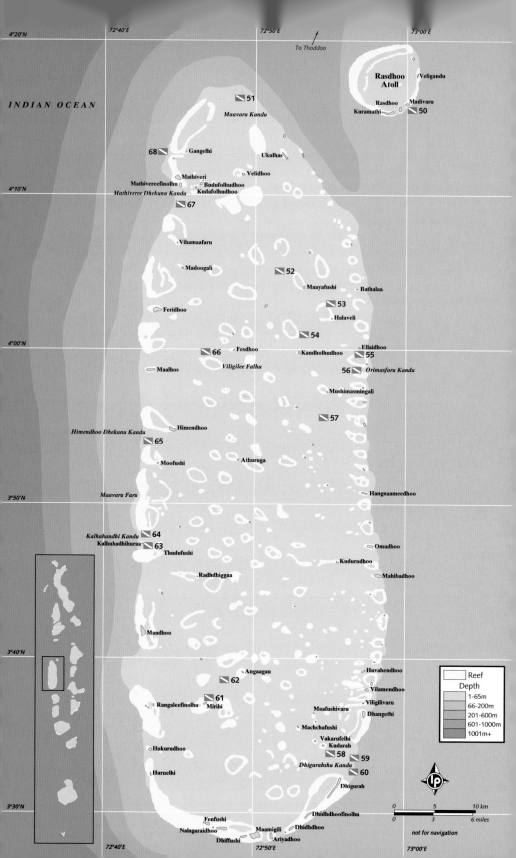

INDIAN OCEAN

4°20'N
72°40'E
72°50'E
73°00'E

Rasdhoo Atoll

Veligandu

51
Maavaru Kandu

Rasdhoo
Kuramathi
Madivaru
50

68
Gangelhi
Ukulhas
Velidhoo

To Thoddoo

Mathiveri
Mathivereefinolhu
Budufolhudhoo
Kudafolhudhoo
Mathiveree Dhekunu Kandu
67

4°10'N

Vihamaafaru

Madoogali
52
Maayafushi
Bathalaa

Feridhoo
53
Halaveli

54
4°00'N
66
Fesdhoo
Kandholhudhoo
Ellaidhoo
55
Maalhos
Viligilee Falhu
56
Orimasfaru Kandu
Mushimasmingali

57

Himendhoo Dhekunu Kandu
Himendhoo
65
Moofushi
Athuruga

3°50'N
Maavaru Faru
Hangnaameedhoo

Kalhahandhi Kandu
64
Kalhuhadhihuraa
63
Omadhoo
Thudufushi
Kudurudhoo
Radhdhiggaa
Mahibadhoo

Mandhoo

3°40'N

Huvahendhoo
Angaagau
62
Vilamendhoo
Viligilivaru
61
Rangaleefinolhu
Mirihi
Maafushivaru
Dhangethi
Machchafushi
Vakarufelhi
Hukurudhoo
Kudarah
58
59
Huruelhi
Dhigurahshu Kandu
60
Dhigurah

3°30'N

Fenfushi
Dhidhdhoofinolhu
Nalaguraidhoo
Maamigili
Dhidhdhoo
Dhiffushi
Ariyadhoo

72°40'E
72°50'E
73°00'E

Reef
Depth
1-65m
66-200m
201-600m
601-1000m
1001m+

0   5   10 km
0   3   6 miles

not for navigation

scattered shallow reef formations prove challenging for navigation. During the southwest monsoon season, reefs on the west side are exposed to heavy waves, and some of the reeftops are quite broken up. This area is also known for its whale shark sightings.

Ari Atoll (Alifu) Dive Sites

	Good Snorkeling	Novice	Intermediate	Advanced
50 Madivaru (Hammerhead Point)			•	
51 Ukulhas Thila				•
52 Maaya Thila		•	•	
53 Halaveli Wreck			•	
54 Kandholhudhoo Thila			•	
55 Ellaidhoo House Reef		•	•	
56 Orimas Thila (Maagaa Thila)		•	•	
57 Fish Head (Mushimasmingali Thila)		•		
58 Kudarah Thila				•
59 Broken Rock			•	
60 Dhigurah Thila			•	
61 Mirihi Madi-Ge		•	•	
62 Angaga Thila		•		
63 Panettone		•		•
64 Thundufushi Thila				•
65 Emas Thila				•
66 Fesdhoo Wreck		•		
67 Miyaruga Thila			•	
68 Gangelhi Kandu		•		•

50 Madivaru (Hammerhead Point)

This spectacular site is well protected from the elements and often boasts excellent visibility. Facing deep water, the narrow channel is home to a school of scalloped hammerheads. The best time to encounter these bizarre-looking sharks is in the early morning on the channel's outside corner, just south of uninhabited Madivaru. To see them up close, swim into the blue a bit, but only if conditions allow.

Location: Rasdhoo Kandu, south end of Rasdhoo Atoll

Depth Range: 10-30m (33-100ft)

Access: Boat or live-aboard

Expertise Rating: Intermediate

The channel features an unusual, complex reef system. A narrow ridge extends from the north wall into the channel, peaking at about 10m. From there it runs seaward, dropping almost vertically. Here you'll find a series of overhangs and caves packed with marine life. Along the ridge you will spot schooling reef fish and pelagics, including barracuda, tuna and jacks, while the channel wall sports many beautiful sea fans.

GAVIN ANDERSON
Scan the blue water to spot scalloped hammerhead sharks.

51 Ukulhas Thila

About 300m long, this thila faces the open ocean, rising from a number of small, submerged reefs on the atoll's outer north rim. It's best known for frequent manta ray sightings during the northeast monsoon season, though there are plenty of other creatures. The site regularly experiences strong currents, and it's generally best to start your dive up-current and drift toward the thila as you descend.

Protruding from the reeftop are several shallow coral heads, which serve as

Location: Maavaru Kandu, north tip of atoll

Depth Range: 13-30m (43-100ft)

Access: Boat or live-aboard

Expertise Rating: Advanced

cleaning stations for the mantas. Also in the shallows, you'll find hovering fusiliers and bluelined snappers. Dense schools of glassfish fill the numerous overhangs, and a number of turtles and morays meander around the thila.

52 Maaya Thila

A protected marine area well inside the atoll, Maaya Thila boasts an incredible abundance and variety of fish. Throughout your dive you'll encounter clouds of butterflyfish, Moorish idols and a several moray eel species, including honeycomb and zebra morays. If you have keen eyes, you may also spot small nudibranchs, as well as camouflaged frogfish and stonefish.

Location: Inside atoll, NW of Maayafushi

Depth Range: 5-35m (16-115ft)

Access: Boat or live-aboard

Expertise Rating: Intermediate

The oval thila is largely undercut, with several coral outcrops to the northwest and one large rock formation at its south tip. Most of the reef features dense and vivid soft-coral growth, and there's a swim-through in the large rock. At the thila's north tip you'll find a large cave frequented by a medley of fish life. You may see barracuda, tuna and batfish or tropical beauties such as lionfish or blue-face angelfish. The cave ceiling is encrusted with bright orange tubastrea coral.

Another highlight of the dive is the large number of white-tip sharks. It's common to find a dozen or more, usually on the side where the current is strongest. Grey reef sharks also patrol the thila.

Currents can be strong, so tuck in close to the thila to avoid being washed off the site. Dive operators commonly tie their boats to a reeftop mooring and provide a rope for controlled descents and ascents. Depending on conditions, divers either return to the boat at the end of the dive or drift off the thila and wait to be picked up.

Spotfin lionfish hunt the reef with venom-filled spines.

53 Halaveli Wreck

This 33m cargo ship was intentionally sunk by management of the Halaveli diving school on New Year's Eve 1990. By now the artificial reef supports a great variety of marine life, particularly soft corals. The wreck sits upright only a short swim from the reef, its keel at 28m and its deck at 20m.

Location: North of Halaveli

Depth Range: 20-28m (65-92ft)

Access: Boat or live-aboard

Expertise Rating: Novice

But this site is perhaps best known for several large resident blotched fantail rays (about 1.5m from wingtip to wingtip) that are regularly fed by the dive school guides. The feeding sessions are very popular and allow divers and photographers a close look at these magnificent animals. The hungry rays can be quite aggressive, so leave the feeding to the instructors, who are familiar with the rays and their habits. Don't try to ride the rays, grab them or reach toward them as they swim above you. Remember, a stingray has a venomous spine near the base of its tail.

The wreck is also home to several large moray eels, groupers, batfish and a host of reef fish. Some of these fish have also learned to take food from divers, so be very cautious, especially around the eels.

Circling the wreck are several large blotched fantail rays, which expect to be fed.

54 Kandholhudhoo Thila

Kandholhudhoo Thila is well inside the atoll and offers an entirely different dive experience than the current-swept kandu dives. This site experiences mostly mild currents and calm surface conditions, making it ideal for novice divers. And although the reef is certainly not the most pristine, especially in the wake of El Niño damage, even experienced divers are drawn here by the unusual fish species.

Location: North of Kandholhudhoo

Depth Range: 8-30m (26-100ft)

Access: Boat or live-aboard

Expertise Rating: Novice

You'll find a variety of juveniles, including yellow boxfish, angelfish and sweetlips, as well as several species of gobies and blennies. If you look carefully, you may spot tiny nudibranchs and camouflaged stonefish, frogfish and leaf scorpionfish. Also keep an eye out for larger creatures such as eagle rays and turtles.

The thila peaks at 8m and slopes gently to 30m. Pinkbar and periophthalma prawn-gobies and their symbiotic partners, blind shrimp, are easy to find along the reef slope. On the east side several caves and overhangs wreathed in

soft corals are home to glassfish, morays and soldierfish.

Leaf scorpionfish mimic debris on the reef.

55 Ellaidhoo House Reef

Blessed with one of the best house reefs in the Maldives, Ellaidhoo resort island is extremely popular with serious divers seeking unlimited diving. The reef consists of a steep, 750m-long wall dotted with caves and rich with marine life.

Location: South side of Ellaidhoo

Depth Range: 1-35m (3-115ft)

Access: Shore

Expertise Rating: Intermediate

The wall is a short swim from the beach or a giant step from the jetty. Most caves are between 10 and 15m, just west of the jetty. Some are barely big enough for a diver to enter, while others are huge, allowing several divers to explore at once. Inside you'll find dense schools of soldierfish, oriental sweetlips, masked

bannerfish and blue-face angelfish, along with morays and lobsters. Many of the caves are also beautifully embellished with large sea fans and crinoids, multihued soft corals and encrusting sponges.

The wall itself is undercut, from 20m to the sandy bottom at 30m. Watch for Napoleonfish and schooling bannerfish, as well as whitetip sharks, tuna and jacks. Stingrays sometimes rest along the sandy bottom.

Closer to the jetty is a small wreck, sunk by the dive center as an added attraction. It rests upside down in 32m, parallel to the wall. Home to several large groupers and a number of moray eels, it's definitely worth a look. In the shallows, snorkelers will enjoy the many parrotfish, schooling tangs and butterflyfish.

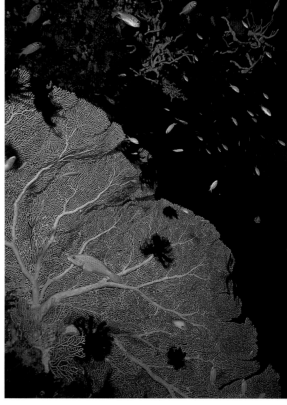

The caves are a short swim west of Ellaidhoo's jetty.

56 Orimas Thila (Maagaa Thila)

A protected marine area, this 100m-long thila sits inside Orimasfaru Kandu, just off the main reef. The steep north side, which faces the channel, is carved with cuts, caves and overhangs. Starting at 6m, a long, narrow crack leads into the thila. This is undoubtedly the most interesting and beautiful area to explore.

A 40m-long cave boasts gorgeous growth, including sea fans, soft corals and black corals. Look for resident soldierfish and bigeyes, as well as the small but photogenic longnose hawkfish, with its distinctive red-and-white pattern, which shelters amid the corals and sea fans. Crimson whip corals, wire corals, lavender rope sponges and multihued encrusting sponges lavishly adorn the sides of the thila. Long-jawed squirrelfish and coral hinds peer out from the

Location: Orimasfaru Kandu

Depth Range: 3-30m (10-100ft)

Access: Boat or live-aboard

Expertise Rating: Intermediate

many crevices, while collared butterflyfish and bluelined snappers gather in schools around the reef.

Along the thila's east side are several coral outcrops split by canyons lined with soft corals. Myriad reef nooks are home to morays, shrimp, gobies, nudibranchs and other colorful critters. Continuing east, you'll find another large cave at 25m, featuring large black coral trees and lots of marine life.

At 6m, the reeftop makes an excellent safety stop and snorkeling spot. You'll see tangs, wrasses, parrotfish and velvety anemones with their symbiotic partner, the Maldives anemonefish. Look carefully to spot lizardfish and scorpionfish.

EDWARD SNIDERS

A favorite among photographers, the longnose hawkfish perches amid black coral deep on the reef.

57 Fish Head (Mushimasmingali Thila)

Considered by many to be one of the best sites in the Maldives, Fish Head is a thrilling thila dive that offers many highlights. Dive operators usually tie off to the thila and use the line for descents and ascents.

Home to a large school of grey reef sharks, this is a great spot to observe these sleek predators. They usually stick to the up-current side of the thila, where they prowl the reef, often closely approaching divers. Ari fishermen traditionally gathered here to catch sharks, but in 1995 the site was declared a protected marine area so divers would be able to encounter the sharks despite the demand for shark fins from the Asian market.

Location: South of Mushimasmingali

Depth Range: 10-40m (33-130ft)

Access: Boat or live-aboard

Expertise Rating: Novice

About 100m long, the oval thila drops steeply to 20m, then flattens out before dropping again to 40m. Protruding from the southeast side is a huge overhang densely packed with bluelined snappers. Caves also dot the north and west sides, where the steep reef wall is deeply undercut between 15 and 30m. This area is thick with sea fans, crinoids and black corals. Watch for clouds of silvery fusiliers, trevallies and circling barracuda throughout your dive, along with several friendly Napoleonfish and a wide range of other reef fish and pelagics.

Long hunted by local fishermen for their fins, grey reef sharks are now protected at Fish Head.

58 Kudarah Thila

Just south of Kudarah resort island, this is another spectacular thila dive. A protected marine area, the thila is about 100m in diameter and can often be circumnavigated in a single dive, except when strong currents are present. Inside the atoll, yet swept by ocean currents from the nearby channel, this thila offers very unusual topography.

Rising from 40 to 12m, four rock pinnacles are deeply carved with undercuts that support fantastic coral gardens. Black coral trees, gorgonian sea fans

Location: Dhigurahshu Kandu

Depth Range: 12-40m (40-130ft)

Access: Boat or live-aboard

Expertise Rating: Advanced

and soft corals line the ceilings. Along the north slope a magnificent forest of gorgonians sways gently in the current. The gullies between the pinnacles are filled with hundreds of bluelined snappers and many other reef fish, including sweetlips, batfish and large groupers. You may also spot small species such as longnose hawkfish, fire dartfish and decorated gobies.

Often in pairs, fire dartfish hover above the seafloor to feed, darting into their burrows if startled.

59 Broken Rock

Broken Rock is in Dhigurahshu Kandu, just northeast of Dhigurah Thila. Marine life highlights include sightings of schooling reef fish, pelagics and turtles, but the main attraction is an amazing canyon that cuts all the way through the thila, from its top at 12m to the bottom at 24m.

The canyon is about 50m long and up to 3m wide. Its sheer walls are fractured with crevices and encrusted with sponges and soft corals, and the canyon is filled with reef fish. Large sea fans and soft corals sprout from the current-exposed thila walls, creating a gorgeous but fragile dive environment, so take care as you

Location: Dhigurahshu Kandu

Depth Range: 12-30m (40-100ft)

Access: Boat or live-aboard

Expertise Rating: Intermediate

make your way around the thila and through the canyon.

To the east is another large rock formation that offers enough of a lee from the current to attract schooling bluelined snappers and barracuda.

60 Dhigurah Thila

In the middle of the almost 5km-wide Dhigurahshu Kandu are several current-swept thilas that attract a profusion of marine life. Sausage-shaped Dhigurah Thila is the largest of these, offering fantastic caves and masses of fish.

Pelagic fish congregate on the north side and northeast corner, where a rocky outcrop extends from the reef. You may

Location: Dhigurahshu Kandu

Depth Range: 10-40m (33-130ft)

Access: Boat or live-aboard

Expertise Rating: Intermediate

see tuna, sharks, rainbow runners and big schools of fusiliers. The entire area is undercut with cave formations. Some are so big, you feel like you're entering a huge house with nature's own designer touches. The ceilings are overgrown with tubastrea and soft corals, while the floors are gardens of crimson sea whips, gorgonian sea fans, crinoids and big black coral trees. Long-jawed squirrelfish, coral hinds, bignose unicornfish, hawkfish and many types of shrimp, gobies and blennies inhabit these massive chambers. Friendly turtles regularly visit the reeftop.

Cute but low on the food chain, pygmy gobies reach 3cm.

61 Mirihi Madi-Ge

Meaning "House of the Rays" in Dhivehi, Madi-Ge is a new wreck on the Mirihi house reef that is indeed home to many friendly pink whiprays and blotched fantail rays. The best time to see the stingrays is in the afternoon, when they gather around the wreck. As the hungry rays can become quite aggressive, they are fed from a dhoni at the surface rather than by hand underwater.

The wreck sits upright on the sand in 22m, right beside the house reef, its

Location: Just offshore, NE of Mirihi

Depth Range: 2-22m (7-72ft)

Access: Shore

Expertise Rating: Novice

deck at about 16m. Divers enter the water from the house reef jetty, a few steps from the dive school. The reef here slopes gently from 2 to 18m. Keep the reef to your right and follow it for about 50m until you see the outline of the wreck.

The 24m former Taiwanese fishing vessel *SN1* was sunk (and renamed) by the Mirihi dive school staff in August 2000. A variety of encrusting sponges, leather and tubastrea corals and a few small soft corals have since taken hold on the wreck. Box crab and dense clouds of glassfish have moved into the holds, while groupers and moray eels roam throughout the ship. Night divers often spot nurse sharks at rest near the wreck, and you may spot a pair of harlequin shrimp in a neighboring coral formation.

This site is suitable for novice divers, as there are no currents to speak of, and snorkelers will enjoy the shallow reef-top, where tropical fish abound. When the visibility is good, snorkelers often spot the stingrays from the surface.

NORBERT PROBST
Fish life on the wreck includes remoras, which attach to the resident rays and clean them of parasites.

62 Angaga Thila

Angaga Thila is well inside the atoll, which means generally easy diving conditions, though visibility may not be as clear as in or near the channels. While coral growth is limited, you'll appreciate this site for its varied marine life.

Location: SW of Angaga

Depth Range: 8-30m (26-100ft)

Access: Boat or live-aboard

Expertise Rating: Novice

The north side of this small, round thila features one large cave, home to groupers, moray eels, lionfish, angelfish

An octopus has excellent vision and is often curious about divers.

and soldierfish. But there are small caves, crevices and overhangs throughout the site. As you meander along the reef wall, you'll likely encounter cornetfish, lots of anemones, parrotfish and butterflyfish, as well as big boys such as whitetip and grey reef sharks, turtles and eagle rays. A number of sea fans and black coral trees thrive in deeper water.

Interesting discoveries also await divers on the shallow reeftop. Keep an eye out for scorpionfish and stonefish, as well as friendly octopuses and many colorful nudibranchs.

63 Panettone

Panettone is the wall alongside Kalha-handhihuraa, a reef that rises from 35m and breaks the surface as a small sand-bank. The wall is carved with crevices, overhangs and caves, including one large cave between 10 and 20m that is adorned in lush soft corals and sea fans. At 30m on the north side you'll find several mushroom-shaped coral heads that reach within 18m of the surface. Sharks,

Location: Kalhahandhi Kandu

Depth Range: 5-35m (16-115ft)

Access: Boat or live-aboard

Expertise Rating: Advanced

barracuda and trevallies frequent these coral-coated pinnacles.

Nutrient-rich currents sweep the channel, enabling corals to flourish along the wall. Feast your eyes on patches of multihued soft corals, tubastrea, crinoid-adorned gorgonians and crimson whip corals. Also watch for pennant and masked bannerfish and Moorish idols. During the northeast monsoon season you may see mantas, drawn here by the abundant plankton.

64 Thundufushi Thila

This large, round thila is in the middle of Kalhahandhi Kandu, where ocean currents provide ideal conditions for a profusion of marine life. Several hundred meters in diameter, this reef boasts fantastic seascapes that are bursting with color.

The best diving is on the north tip of the thila, facing the inside of the atoll and Maavaru Faru, the reef north of the channel. Here the thila drops in large steps to the channel floor, with several coral rocks stacked on a ledge at 25m. Soft corals are abundant, as are glassfish, masked bannerfish, Moorish idols and tangs. Between the ledge and the reef-top are numerous overhangs that shelter

Location: Kalhahandhi Kandu

Depth Range: 10-35m (33-115ft)

Access: Boat or live-aboard

Expertise Rating: Advanced

soldierfish, long-jawed squirrelfish and the occasional resting nurse shark. Sea fans, crinoids, whip corals and soft corals adorn most of the wall, and schooling fusiliers and eagle rays cruise the reeftop.

Look into the blue of the channel and you may see sharks and jacks. Mantas visit during the northeast monsoon season.

Nocturnal soldierfish need big eyes to navigate in caves during the day and on the reef at night.

65 Emas Thila

Rising from the channel floor between Moofushi and Himendhoo, Emas Thila is a 1km-long, sausage-shaped thila that serves as a gathering place for manta rays during the northeast monsoon season. These graceful creatures frequent the shallow reeftop between 10 and 15m, where they often approach divers quite closely. Although the mantas are a highlight of the dive, there's a lot more to see.

Location: Himendhoo Dhekunu Kandu

Depth Range: 10-30m (33-100ft)

Access: Boat or live-aboard

Expertise Rating: Advanced

Most of the thila is undercut with caves, but the formations are particularly spectacular on the southwest corner. Facing the open ocean, the steep wall is carved with a series of dramatic overhangs from 30m to the reeftop. Decorated with sea fans, tubastrea and whip corals, these chambers are filled with many fish and invertebrate species.

This chiseled wall stretches for several hundred meters along the south side of the thila, a ledge extending from the wall at 30m. Along the ledge sit coral heads sculpted into arches and ravines, all blanketed in vivid soft corals and sponges. Divers and photographers will find schooling oriental sweetlips, collared butterflyfish, masked bannerfish and schooling snappers. You'll also see Napoleonfish, large schools of pennant bannerfish and clouds of swirling anthias. This is a fantastic dive, but currents are often strong, making the safety stop in mid-water difficult.

Among the schooling fish that gather here are yellowspot emperors, which disperse at night to feed.

66 | Fesdhoo Wreck

This dive centers on the wreck of a former fishing trawler that now serves as an excellent artificial reef. A short swim west is an active thila that tops out at 12m.

The trawler is 30m long and rests at 30m. Its hull is encrusted with tubastrea, black and soft corals, sponges, feathery hydroids and hard corals. You'll find clouds of glassfish and anthias throughout the wreckage, along with butterflyfish, parrotfish, lionfish, many different wrasses, large groupers and moray eels. If you look carefully, you'll also discover tiny

Location: North of Viligilee Falhu

Depth Range: 12-30m (40-100ft)

Access: Boat or live-aboard

Expertise Rating: Novice

blennies and gobies, as well as the many nudibranchs that feed on the wreck's encrusting sponges. A large school of batfish often hovers off the stern.

67 | Miyaruga Thila

This relatively small but spectacular thila is a photographer's dream. Starting at 15m, the largely undercut reef drops to about 25m. The entire thila is carved with undercuts that are home to unicornfish, soldierfish, a variety of moray eels, and the occasional clown triggerfish and coral hind. If you look carefully, you may also spot small cleaner shrimp or gobies near the undercuts.

Toward the north side of the thila are two tunnels that start just below 20m and cut all the way through the rock. Both tunnels are filled with soldierfish and fusiliers, and both start and end inside large undercuts adorned with encrusting sponges and colorful soft corals.

Southwest of the thila are several coral heads, two of them forming a narrow channel between the rocks and the thila. Photographers should go in search of the giant morays, soft corals and sponges among the rocks.

Location: Mathiveree Dhekunu Kandu

Depth Range: 15-25m (50-82ft)

Access: Boat or live-aboard

Expertise Rating: Intermediate

Lacking gill covers, morays must breathe openmouthed.

68 Gangelhi Kandu

At 2.5km long, Gangelhi Kandu is the longest channel in the Maldives. The site is best dived with an incoming current, allowing you to enter the water on one of the outside corners, then drift into the channel.

Location: West of Gangelhi

Depth Range: 5-40m (16-130ft)

Access: Boat or live-aboard

Expertise Rating: Advanced

The walls of the channel are equally worth exploring, with lots of reef fish and large schools of redtooth triggerfish. On the north side a long cave runs between 15 and 20m and is home to large groupers and stingrays. Hawksbill turtles frequent the reeftop, while Napoleonfish appear to be seasonal and are usually present during the southwest monsoon season. During the northeast monsoon season, when the current often flows out of the atoll, divers encounter large numbers of manta rays near the surface.

Endangered hawksbills are protected in the Maldives, and it's illegal to sell or export turtle-shell products.

South & North Maalhosmadulu Atolls (Baa & Raa) Dive Sites

These neighboring atolls in the northern half of the archipelago were only recently opened to tourism. The administrative district of Baa includes both South Maalhosmadulu and the smaller Goidhoo Atoll to the south. South Maalhosmadulu is 42km (26 miles) long and 32km (20 miles) wide. There are 41 uninhabited islands in the atoll, five of which have been developed into resorts, the first opening its doors in 1995. The atoll's 10,000 residents are spread out over 10 islands. Their principal occupation is fishing, though local craftspeople are also known for producing the quality lacquerwork sold in souvenir shops.

The reefs in Baa remain pristine, with several kandus and plenty of great thila dives, both in the channels and inside the atoll. During the southwest monsoon season, particularly between May and July, divers often encounter mantas and whale sharks.

Largely unexplored, North Maalhosmadulu is 65km (40 miles) long and 28km (17 miles) wide, encompassing more than 90 islands. While 16 islands are locally inhabited, boasting a population of more than 12,500, only one island has been designated as a tourist resort. The atoll's greatest claim to fame remains its strong boatbuilding tradition. Alifushi is the teaching center of the art of boatbuilding, and Ugoofaaru, the capital island, is home to the largest fishing fleet in the country.

The diving is spectacular. Numerous channels separate the islands and reefs along the atoll's perimeter, while the inner lagoon is studded with thilas and giris of all sizes. Overall, it's considered a destination for advanced divers. Currents are typically stronger here than elsewhere in the Maldives, as the lagoon seafloor averages about 20m (65ft) shallower than at other atolls.

As at Coco Palm, overwater bungalows are a popular lodging option at several Maldives resorts.

South & North Maalhosmadulu Atolls (Baa & Raa) Dive Sites

	Good Snorkeling	Novice	Intermediate	Advanced
69 Horubadhoo Thila (Dhigali Haa)		●		
70 Dharavandhoo Thila		●		
71 Beriyan Faru Thila				●
72 Kottefaru Kuda Thila				●
73 Vaadhoo Thila				●

The Biggest Fish in the Sea

Growing to whale-like proportions of 12m (40ft) long, the whale shark (*Rhincodon typus*) is the world's largest fish. Despite their size, however, whale sharks lead docile lives. They spend much of their time swimming placidly near the surface, feeding on plankton, small fish and crustaceans, which they strain from the water with specialized teeth and gill rakers.

Although chance encounters are possible in tropical waters worldwide, whale sharks are more common in certain areas during certain times of the year. In the Maldives the northeast monsoon season (December through March) brings currents that flush plankton-rich lagoon water onto the reefs along the west side of the atolls, in turn attracting whale sharks. Divers often spot these gentle giants from the boat, as they typically float near the surface. Their white-spotted checkerboard pattern is easily recognizable. When conditions allow, the boat driver may permit divers to enter the water wearing a mask, snorkel and fins, though some drivers fear the whale shark may capsize the dhoni.

Underwater, your first impression of the whale shark may be a sudden total eclipse of the sun as the massive animal passes overhead. Though generally indifferent toward divers and snorkelers, whale sharks will occasionally take an interest in the boat, perhaps bumping or brushing against the hull. Such visits may last several hours.

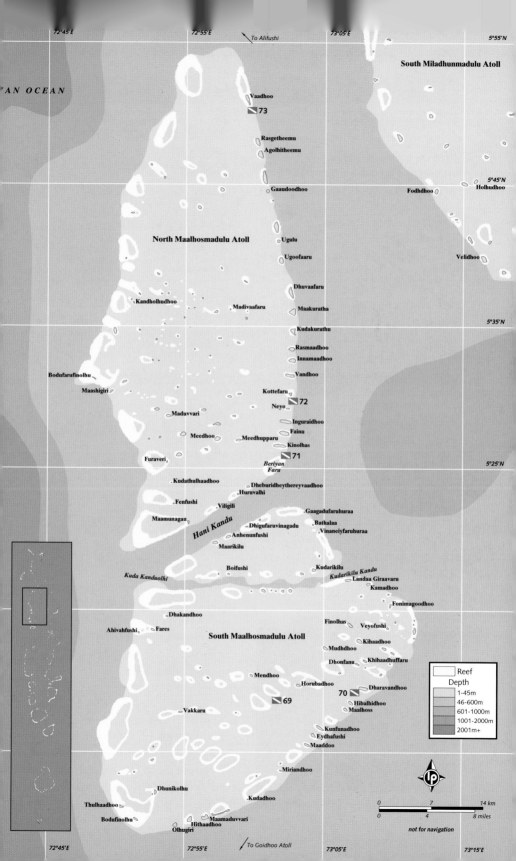

69 Horubadhoo Thila (Dhigali Haa)

About 100m long, this thila was declared a protected marine area to safeguard the grey reef sharks and other pelagics that frequent the site. Isolated from other reefs, the thila drops from 10m to a large sandy expanse at 40m. The formation is carved with small caves and overhangs filled with soldierfish.

The highlight of the dive, however, is the abundance of pelagics and schooling fish. You'll spot grey reef sharks and eagle rays during the northeast monsoon season, along with schools of batfish, barracuda and fusiliers that swirl around and above the reef. Two canyons cut through

Location: South Maalhosmadulu, inside atoll, SW of Horubadhoo

Depth Range: 10-40m+ (33-130ft+)

Access: Boat or live-aboard

Expertise Rating: Intermediate

the thila from north to south, sheltering a profusion of colorful soft corals.

70 Dharavandhoo Thila

This site is one of the prettiest and most colorful in the area. From Dharavandhoo this narrow thila extends south some 300m, widening to about 60m across its middle. The reeftop lies between 5 and 20m.

Along the thila's sides you'll discover a number of ledges, overhangs and caves, many lined with tubastrea coral, sea whips and dense accumulations of black coral. Vibrant sponges, crinoids and sea

Location: South Maalhosmadulu, SW of Dharavandhoo

Depth Range: 5-40m (16-130ft)

Access: Boat or live-aboard

Expertise Rating: Intermediate

fans add a splash of color. Toward the south end of the thila, soft-coral trees sprout from the reef wall. From the sandy seafloor at 40m several coral structures rise to between 35 and 30m, attracting lots of schooling fish.

The reeftop serves as a manta cleaning station during the southwest monsoon season, while reef sharks patrol the area year-round. Divers with a keen eye for small creatures may spot leaf scorpionfish or even the elusive harlequin ghost pipefish, which often hides within the tentacles of crinoids.

Harlequin ghost pipefish are able to change color.

71 Beriyan Faru Thila

Start your dive by exploring the outside wall of Beriyan Faru. The reeftop rises as shallow as 3m and is home to camouflaged scorpionfish, grazing tangs and many invertebrates. Down the sheer wall you may spot patrolling reef sharks, schooling jacks or curious Napoleonfish. From the corner of the reef it's a short swim to this thila just inside the channel.

Location: North Maalhosmadulu, south of Kinolhas

Depth Range: 3-30m (10-100ft)

Access: Boat or live-aboard

Expertise Rating: Advanced

Easily circumnavigated, the thila is embellished with brightly colored soft corals and sponges. The caves and overhangs in particular are densely lined with tubastrea and soft corals. Amid this profusion of color you'll find large unicornfish, sweetlips, long-jawed squirrelfish and countless other fish and invertebrate species.

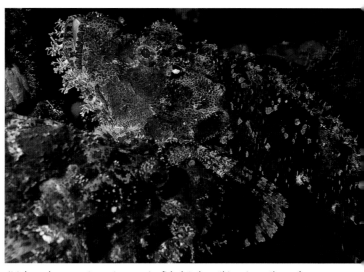

It takes a keen eye to spot a scorpionfish, let alone this pair, on the reef.

72 Kottefaru Kuda Thila

This relatively shallow thila is a fantastic site. The thila is laced with numerous crevices, caves and overhangs. Packed with marine life, they offer great photo opportunities and are fun to explore. The thila's sides host multicolored soft corals, while the reeftop is endowed with countless magnificent anemones. Descend to the sandy seafloor at 35m to find several goby species and the occasional stingray.

Glance into the blue for a glimpse at dense clouds of jacks and barracuda.

Location: North Maalhosmadulu, south of Kottefaru

Depth Range: 6-35m (20-115ft)

Access: Boat or live-aboard

Expertise Rating: Advanced

Mantas may visit during the southwest monsoon season.

73 Vaadhoo Thila

Powerful currents sweep this site in the wide channel south of Vaadhoo, ensuring active fish and healthy coral growth. The dive centers on a large thila that drops from 12m to just below the sport-diving limit. Take your time exploring the thila, as it's easily circumnavigated in one dive.

The south side of the thila is carved with caves and overhangs of all sizes. Blanketed in soft corals, the formations house long-jawed squirrelfish, soldierfish, moray eels, mollusks and crustaceans.

Large schools of jacks, fusiliers and other pelagics swirl in the water column

Location: North Maalhosmadulu, south of Vaadhoo

Depth Range: 12-30m (40-100ft)

Access: Boat or live-aboard

Expertise Rating: Advanced

around the thila, as do bluelined snappers and large unicornfish. The reeftop at 12m is a good place to find parrotfish, butterflyfish and tangs.

In a scene repeated throughout the Maldives, reef species thrive here amid multicolored soft corals.

Faadhippolhu Atoll (Lhaviyani) Dive Sites

Faadhippolhu is 35km (22 miles) long and 37km (23 miles) wide. The atoll comprises more than 50 islands, of which only five are locally inhabited and four have been developed into tourist resorts. The first resort opened in 1988 and was the atoll's sole accommodation until 1999. Faadhippolhu's 8,000 residents are known for their fishing skills and local medicinal expertise, as well as for designing handicrafts from coral and mother-of-pearl.

The atoll's southeast side features a 30km-long stretch of reef, uninterrupted by channels, while the remaining barrier reef is carved with numerous channels, many of which are quite narrow. There are few thilas or other reef formations inside the atoll, hence most diving is done in the current-swept channels.

Locals on Naifaru, the atoll's capital island, design handicrafts from coral and mother-of-pearl.

119

Faadhippolhu Atoll (Lhaviyani)

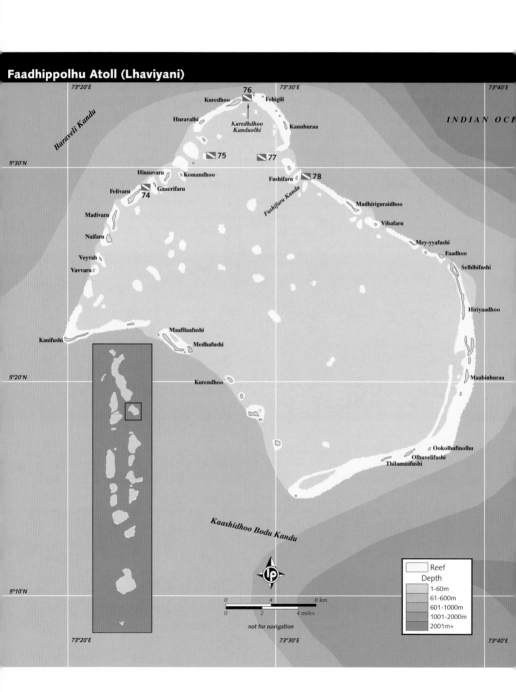

73°20'E

73°30'E

73°40'E

Baraveli Kandu

76

Kuredhoo · Fehigili

Huravalhi

Kuredhdhoo Kanduolhi

Kanuhuraa

INDIAN OCE

5°30'N

▧ **75**

▧ **77**

Hinnavaru · Komandhoo

Fushifaru ⏍ ◣**78**

Felivaru · Gaaerifaru

74

Fushifaru Kandu

Madhiriguraidhoo

Madivaru

Vihafaru

Naifaru

Mey-yyafushi

Faadhoo

Veyvah

Selhlhifushi

Vavvaru

Hiriyaadhoo

Maafilaafushi

Kanifushi

Medhafushi

5°20'N

Kurendhoo

Maabinhuraa

⌀ Ookolhufinolhu

Olhuvelifushi

Thilamaafushi

Kaashidhoo Bodu Kandu

5°10'N

🧭

	Reef
	Depth
	1-60m
	61-600m
	601-1000m
	1001-2000m
	2001m+

0   4   8 km

0   2   4 miles

not for navigation

73°20'E

73°30'E

73°40'E

Faadhippolhu Atoll (Lhaviyani) Dive Sites

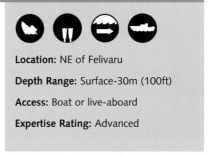

	Good Snorkeling	Novice	Intermediate	Advanced
74 Shipyard (Graveyard)				●
75 Narcola Giri	●	●		
76 Kuredhoo Express				●
77 Maa Giri		●	●	
78 Fushifaru Thila		●		●

74 Shipyard (Graveyard)

The highlight of this dive is a pair of shipwrecks that rest in the channel separating Felivaru and Gaaerifaru. Strong currents often sweep the channel, and penetration of either wreck should be approached with caution.

Location: NE of Felivaru

Depth Range: Surface-30m (100ft)

Access: Boat or live-aboard

Expertise Rating: Advanced

Skipjack II was the mother ship of the Felivaru fish factory until 1985, when plans were made to scuttle the ship at sea. However, as workers were preparing her for sinking, she caught fire. For safety reasons, the ship was cut loose and allowed to sink in the channel. She now rests vertically on her stern at 30m, leaning against the reef. Marking the dive site, her bow rises high out of the water and is easy to see from a distance.

Gaafaru also belonged to the fish factory and was later sunk in the same location, a short drift southeast of the *Skipjack II*. She lies on her port side at 30m, her starboard side topping out at 22m.

Both wrecks support extensive soft-coral growth and an amazing variety of marine life. Residents include nudibranchs, flatworms, morays, lionfish, hawkfish and gobies, while a friendly school of batfish shuttles back and forth

A nudibranch's defenses include its bitter taste.

between the ships. Photographers should keep an eye out for butterflyfish, emperor and Indian yellowtail angelfish, and juvenile and adult boxfish.

75 Narcola Giri

This small, elongated giri drops steeply and is carved throughout with overhangs

Location: Inside atoll, south of Huravalhi

Depth Range: 3-30m (10-100ft)

Access: Boat or live-aboard

Expertise Rating: Novice

Watch for large stingrays along the north wall.

and crevices, though the northern side boasts the best diving. You may surprise a blotched fantail ray among the many anemones and sea fans, while other stingrays, garden eels, prawn-gobies and the occasional zebra shark swim along the sandy seafloor at 30m. Snorkelers will appreciate the array of tropical fish on the shallow reeftop, including tangs, parrotfish and fast-swimming wrasses.

On the west side, several coral pinnacles rise from the seafloor, attracting many species of reef fish, including butterflyfish, parrotfish, wrasses and tangs. Also look for juvenile angelfish, yellow boxfish, scorpionfish and lionfish.

76 Kuredhoo Express

A protected marine area, this thrilling drift dive is through a channel that faces the open ocean. The east outside corner of the channel drops in big steps to 30m. Between 25 and 30m are many beautiful overhangs and caves, most blanketed in lush soft corals and packed with soldierfish and long-jawed squirrelfish. Drop to the deepest point and you'll probably encounter big schools of black snappers

Location: Kuredhoo Kanduolhi

Depth Range: 5-35m (16-115ft)

Access: Boat or live-aboard

Expertise Rating: Advanced

and jacks, as well as sharks, barracuda and perhaps eagle rays.

In the middle of the channel mouth, at 35m, you'll find a huge cavern, its ceiling decorated with orange tubastrea and bluish soft coral. Once inside the channel, keep the wall to your left and

you'll soon discover a number of smaller overhangs. Scan the channel floor to spot several species of gobies and larger animals such as stingrays. To end your dive, slowly make your way to the shallows atop the wall, a few meters below the surface.

At Kuredhoo Express, schooling black snappers face into the current like a rain of sleek bombs.

77 Maa Giri

Just inside the wide channel south of Kanuhuraa, this flower-shaped giri is bathed in currents that support myriad marine life. You can dive here on either an incoming or outgoing current by simply reversing the entry point.

The topography varies, ranging from a staircase of ledges to steep walls coated with leather coral. Throughout the giri you'll find crevices and overhangs that shelter morays, crustaceans, coral hinds and other critters. Dozens of anemones

Location: SW of Kanuhuraa

Depth Range: 5-20m (16-65m)

Access: Boat or live-aboard

Expertise Rating: Novice

make their home on this small, round reef, and you'll also see jacks and fusiliers, parrotfish and oriental sweetlips.

78 Fushifaru Thila

This stunning, challenging site lies in mid-channel at the mouth of Fushifaru Kandu. The dive centers on a 200m-long thila that has been declared a protected marine area. Ideally, divers enter on a weak incoming current, though currents are often ferocious in the channel, and advanced diving skills are a must. The currents here sustain a wealth of marine life.

Location: Fushifaru Kandu

Depth Range: 10-25m (33-82ft)

Access: Boat or live-aboard

Expertise Rating: Advanced

The thila rises from the channel floor at about 25m and tops out between 10 and 15m. Atop the thila you'll find numerous cleaning stations manned by cleaner wrasses, which groom morays, unicornfish, coral hinds and many other customers. Look amid the sand around the base of the thila to find stingrays and resting whitetip sharks, as well as small creatures such as triplefins and gobies.

The thila is abloom with vivid soft corals, often obscured by clouds of glassfish, snappers, oriental sweetlips and collared butterflyfish. You're also likely to encounter foraging turtles, a variety of moray eels and friendly Napoleonfish. The northeast side faces the drop-off into the abyss, the best place to spot grey reef sharks, hammerheads, barracuda, eagle rays and other exciting pelagic species.

Turtles & Tourists

Few dive destinations in the world are home to turtles as friendly as those in the Maldives. Divers are able to get literally nose to beak with the ones that live here on protected reefs. While massive loggerhead and leatherback turtles still exist in the region, they are rarely seen. Those most commonly encountered are the green sea turtle and the hawksbill, easily identified by its distinctive, bird-like beak (see photo).

For centuries turtles have been hunted for their flesh and shells. While the collection of sea turtles and the sale and export of turtle-shell products is now forbidden in the Maldives, souvenirs such as combs, bracelets and other ornaments made from turtle shell are still sold locally. As long as tourists continue to buy these banned products, islanders will continue to illegally hunt the turtles for profit. Unfortunately, turtle flesh and eggs also remain popular, all contributing to a decline in turtle numbers.

Marine Life

The Maldives is home to more than 700 fish species and a wide variety of invertebrates. Although a few species are endemic to the archipelago, many are also found in the Arabian and Red Seas, and some are as widespread as the tropical Pacific. This section identifies some of the species divers will likely encounter in the Maldives.

MICHAEL AW

While coral bleaching has damaged the shallow hard-coral gardens (see "Coral Bleaching," page 131), the reefs still sport multi-colored soft corals, sponges and anemones. The buildup of algae on the coral skeletons has also led to a boom in the numbers of herbivorous reef fish, a colorful and active population sure to thrill snorkelers and divers alike.

Keep in mind that common names are used freely by most divers and are often inconsistent. The two-part scientific name is more precise. This system is known as binomial nomenclature—the method of using two words (shown in italics) to identify an organism. The first italic word is the genus, into which members of similar species are grouped. The second word, the species, refers to a recognizable group within a genus whose members are capable of interbreeding. Where the species is unknown or not yet named, the genus name is followed by *sp.*

Common Vertebrates

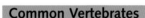

long-jawed squirrelfish
Sargocentron spiniferum

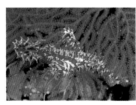
harlequin ghost pipefish
Solenostomus paradoxus

red-cheeked pipefish
Corythoichthys sp.

coral hind
Cephalopholis miniata

saddleback coralgrouper
Plectropomus laevis

freckled hawkfish
Paracirrhites forsteri

longnose hawkfish
Oxycirrhites typus

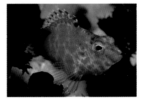

pixy hawkfish
Cirrhitichthys oxycephalus

bluelined snapper
Lutjanus kasmira

bluestreak fusilier
Pterocaesio tile

oriental sweetlips
Plectorhinchus vittatus

teardrop butterflyfish
Chaetodon unimaculatus

yellowhead butterflyfish
Chaetodon xanthocephalus

collared butterflyfish
Chaetodon collare

Indian butterflyfish
Chaetodon mitratus

longfin bannerfish
Heniochus acuminatus

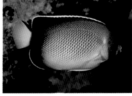

Indian yellowtail angelfish
Apolemichthys xanthurus

blue-face angelfish
Pomacanthus xanthometopon

emperor angelfish
Pomacanthus imperator

Maldives anemonefish
Amphiprion nigripes

Napoleonfish (humphead wrasse)
Cheilinus undulatus

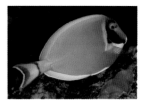

fire dartfish
Nemateleotris magnifica

beautiful prawn-goby
Amblyeleotris aurora

powder-blue surgeonfish
Acanthurus leucosternon

bignose unicornfish
Naso vlamingi

stellate rabbitfish
Siganus s. stellatus

clown triggerfish
Balistoides conspicillum

Common Invertebrates

sea squirt
Didemnum molle

orange cup coral
Tubastraea coccinea

Maldives sponge snail
Coriocella hibyae

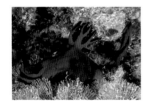

nudibranch
Tambja morosa

cuttlefish
Sepia latimanus

octopus
Octopus cyanea

mantis shrimp
Odontodactylus scyllarus

harlequin shrimp
Hymenocera picta

feather star
Crinoid sp.

Hazardous Marine Life

Marine animals almost never attack divers, but many have defensive and offensive weaponry that can be triggered if they feel threatened or annoyed. The ability to recognize hazardous creatures is a valuable asset in avoiding injury. Following are some of the potentially hazardous creatures most commonly found in the Maldives.

Cone Shell

Do not touch or pick up cone shells. Found generally on the ocean floor amid sand or rubble, often partially buried, these mollusks deliver a venomous sting by shooting a tiny poison dart from their funnel-like proboscis. Stings will cause numbness and can be followed by muscular paralysis or even respiratory paralysis and heart failure. Immobilize the victim, apply a pressure bandage, be prepared to use CPR, and seek urgent medical aid.

Stonefish

Stonefish, scorpionfish and lionfish all inject venom through dorsal spines that can penetrate booties, wetsuits and gloves. They typically rest quietly on the bottom or on coral, looking more like rocks. To avoid injury, practice good buoyancy control and watch where you put your hands. Wounds typically cause intense throbbing pain. Soak the wound in nonscalding hot vinegar or water for 30 to 90 minutes. Victims who experience more serious allergic reactions, such as convulsions or cardiorespiratory failure, should be transported to a hospital immediately.

Moray Eel

Distinguished by their long, thick, snake-like bodies and tapered heads, moray eels come in a variety of colors and patterns. Normally, eels are shy and retreat upon divers' approach. Don't feed them or put your hand in a dark hole—eels have the unfortunate combination of sharp teeth and poor eyesight and will bite if they feel threatened. If you are bitten, don't try to pull your hand away suddenly—a moray's teeth slant backward and are extraordinarily sharp. Let the eel release your hand and then surface slowly. Treat with antiseptics, anti-tetanus and antibiotics.

Crown-of-Thorns

This large sea star may have up to 23 arms, although 13 to 18 are more commonly observed. Body coloration can be blue, green or grayish with spines tinted red or orange. The spines are venomous and can deliver a painful sting even if the animal has been dead for two or three days. Also beware the toxic pedicellariae (pincers) between the spines, which can also cause severe pain upon contact. To treat stings, remove any loose spines, soak stung area in nonscalding hot water for 30 to 90 minutes and seek medical aid. Neglected wounds may produce serious injury. If you've been stung before, your reaction to another sting may be worse than the first.

Jellyfish

Jellyfish sting by releasing nematocysts, stinging cells contained in their trailing tentacles. As a rule, the longer the tentacles, the more painful the sting. Stings are often just irritating, not painful, but should be treated immediately with a de-

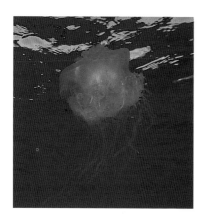

contaminant such as vinegar, rubbing alcohol, baking soda, papain or dilute household ammonia. A far greater problem is the Portuguese man-of-war, a distant cousin of the jellyfish that floats at the surface and has very long trailing tentacles. Sting symptoms range from a mild itch to intense pain, blistering, skin discoloration, shock, breathing difficulties and even unconsciousness. Remove the tentacles, preferably with tweezers, though anything but bare hands will do. Some people may have a stronger reaction than others, in which case you should prepare to resuscitate and seek medical aid.

Fire Coral

Although often mistaken for stony coral, fire coral is a hydroid colony that secretes a hard, calcareous skeleton. Fire coral grows in many different shapes, often encrusting or taking the form of a variety of reef structures. It's usually identifiable by its tan, mustard or brown color and finger-like columns with whitish tips. The entire colony is covered by tiny pores and fine, hair-like projections nearly invisible to the unaided eye. Fire coral "stings" by discharging small, specialized cells called

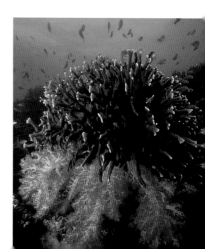

nematocysts. Contact causes a burning sensation that lasts for several minutes and may produce red welts on the skin. Do not rub the area, as you'll only spread the stinging particles. Cortisone cream can reduce the inflammation, and antihistamine cream is good for killing the pain. A doctor should treat serious stings.

Sea Snake

Air-breathing reptiles with venom that's 20 times stronger than any land snake, sea snakes release venom only when feeding or under extreme distress—so most defensive bites don't contain venom. Sea snakes rarely bite even if they are handled, but avoid touching  them. To treat a sea snake bite, use a pressure bandage and immobilize the victim. Try to identify the snake, be prepared to administer CPR, and seek urgent medical aid.

Shark

Sharks come in many shapes and sizes (see "Watching Sharks," page 83). They are most recognizable by their triangular dorsal fin. Though many species are shy, there are occasional attacks. About 25 species worldwide are considered dangerous to humans. Sharks will generally not attack unless provoked, so don't taunt, tease or feed them. Avoid spearfishing, carrying fish baits or mimicking a wounded fish, and your likelihood of being attacked will greatly diminish. Face and quietly watch any shark that is acting aggressively and be prepared to push it away with a camera, knife or tank. If someone is bitten by a shark, stop the bleeding, reassure the patient, treat for shock and seek immediate medical aid.

Diving Conservation & Awareness

EDWARD SNIJDERS

The Maldives has long been known for some of the healthiest, most prolific reefs in the world. But those reefs face a growing threat from a number of natural and manmade factors, including coral bleaching, overfishing, shark finning, coral mining and pollution. Fortunately, local dive operators are working in concert with the Maldives government to safeguard the marine environment.

Moorings have been installed, and artificial reefs (wrecks) are encouraged. The government has designated several protected marine areas to spare certain reef species from overharvesting, and new resorts face stringent environmental restrictions. It's an uphill battle, though, as the local population continues to grow, sea levels rise and the Asian market tempts local fishermen with high prices for threatened marine species.

Coral Bleaching

As temperature-sensitive organisms, corals can only function within a narrow temperature range. But during a particularly severe El Niño in March 1998, average water temperatures rose suddenly from 27 to 32°C (81 to 90°F), inflicting significant damage to the Maldives' shallow hard-coral gardens. The stressed corals began to expel microscopic zooxanthellae, life-supporting symbiotic algae, from their tissues. As the algae also contribute color to the reef, the affected corals turn white when zooxanthellae disappear, a phenomenon known as coral bleaching. If warm water conditions persist for too long, the coral polyps eventually die off.

While it took barely two weeks for coral bleaching to wipe out up to 90% of the Maldives' magnificent hard-coral gardens, it will take many years for the reefs to fully rebound. However, the recovery process has already begun, and tiny new polyps are already visible. Scientists are learning from the process and hope that new technologies being tested in the Maldives will assist them in reef recovery efforts worldwide.

Marine Reserves & Regulations

Due to overfishing, the Maldives government has established 25 protected marine areas within the tourist atolls. At these sites it's illegal to anchor, dump any trash, mine for coral and sand, collect, fish or harass any type of marine life (including sharks), as well as engage in any other activities that may damage the reef or its inhabitants. The diving community has lobbied for additional protected marine areas.

The government has also banned the collection and export of a variety of threatened species, including turtles and all turtle-shell products and most coral and shell products. It's even illegal to remove shells or coral either from beaches or during dives. Violators face hefty fines.

Sea cucumbers, the natural vacuum cleaners of the ocean floor, have long been victims of commercial overfishing. A ban on the use of scuba for sea cucumber collection should allow their numbers to regenerate in deeper waters.

In recent years, groupers and Napoleonfish were hunted mercilessly, as the Asian market was paying Maldivian fishermen extremely high prices for the fish. Since demand peaked in 1995, the export of either species has been entirely banned. Also threatened by commercial fishing, giant clams have been protected since 1991.

Another major concern is waste disposal. In the past, waste materials were mostly comprised of coconut products, and everything was dumped in the sea. But due to the widespread import of packaged goods by even the more traditional villages, waste management has become a serious issue. Tourist resorts are required to use compactors and incinerators, and all garbage from Male' is disposed of at Thilafushi, a nearby island that serves specifically as a garbage dump.

JAMES LYON

Also known as "Trash Island," Thilafushi is home to a garbage dump and a cement factory.

Responsible Diving

Dive sites are often along reefs and walls covered in beautiful corals and sponges. It only takes a moment—an inadvertently placed hand or knee, or a careless brush or kick with a fin—to destroy this fragile, living part of our delicate ecosystem. By following certain basic guidelines while diving, you can help preserve the ecology and beauty of the reefs:

1. Never drop boat anchors onto a coral reef and take care not to ground boats on coral. Encourage dive operators and regulatory bodies in their efforts to establish permanent moorings at appropriate dive sites.

2. Practice and maintain proper buoyancy control and avoid overweighting. Be aware that your buoyancy can change over the period of an extended trip. Initially you may breathe harder and need more weighting; a few days later you may breathe more easily and need less weight. Tip: Use your weight belt and tank position to maintain a horizontal position—raise them to elevate your feet, lower them to elevate your upper body. Also be careful about buoyancy loss: As you dive deeper, your wetsuit compresses, as does the air in your BC.

3. Avoid touching living marine organisms with your body and equipment. Polyps can be damaged by even the gentlest contact. Never stand on or touch living coral. The use of gloves is no longer recommended: Gloves make it too easy to hold on to the reef. The abrasion caused by gloves may be even more damaging to the reef than your hands. If you must hold on to the reef, touch only exposed rock or dead coral.

4. Take great care in underwater caves. Spend as little time within them as possible, as your air bubbles can damage fragile organisms. Divers should take turns inspecting the interiors of small caves or under ledges to lessen the chances of damaging contact.

5. Be conscious of your fins. Even without contact, the surge from heavy fin strokes near the reef can do damage. Avoid full-leg kicks when diving close to the bottom and when leaving a photo scene. When you inadvertently kick something, stop kicking! It seems obvious, but some divers either panic or are totally oblivious when they bump something. When treading water in shallow reef areas, take care not to kick up clouds of sand. Settling sand can smother the delicate reef organisms.

6. Secure gauges, computer consoles and the octopus regulator so they're not dangling—they are like miniature wrecking balls to a reef.

7. When swimming in strong currents, be extra careful about leg kicks and handholds.

8. Photographers should take extra precautions, as cameras and equipment affect buoyancy. Changing f-stops, framing a subject and maintaining position for a photo often conspire to thwart the ideal "no-touch" approach on a reef. When you must use "holdfasts," choose them intelligently (i.e., use one finger only for leverage off an area of dead coral).

9. Resist the temptation to collect or buy coral or shells. Aside from the ecological damage, collection of marine souvenirs depletes the beauty of a site and spoils other divers' enjoyment. The same goes for marine archaeological sites (mainly shipwrecks). Respect their integrity. Some sites are even protected from looting by law.

10. Ensure that you take home all your trash and any litter you may find as well. Plastics in particular pose a serious threat to marine life.

11. Resist the temptation to feed fish. You may disturb their normal eating habits, encourage aggressive behavior or feed them food that is detrimental to their health.

12. Minimize your disturbance of marine animals. Don't ride on the backs of turtles or manta rays, as this can cause them great anxiety.

Resist the urge to take home marine souvenirs.

Marine Conservation Organizations

Coral reefs and oceans are facing unprecedented environmental pressures. The following groups are actively involved in promoting responsible diving practices, publicizing environmental marine threats and lobbying for better policies:

CEDAM International
☎ 914-271-5365
www.cedam.org

CORAL: The Coral Reef Alliance
☎ 510-848-0110
www.coralreefalliance.org

Cousteau Society
☎ 757-523-9335
www.cousteau.org

Project AWARE Foundation
☎ 949-858-7657
www.padi.com/aware

ReefKeeper International
☎ 305-358-4600
www.reefkeeper.org

Reef Relief
☎ 305-294-3100
www.reefrelief.org

Listings

Telephone Calls

To call the Maldives, dial the international access code for the country you are calling from (in the U.S. it's 011) + 960 (the Maldives' country code) + the 6-digit local number.

Safari Dive Boats

More than 90 safari dive boats (live-aboards) are registered with the Maldives Ministry of Tourism. While some simply offer relaxing sightseeing cruises, the vessels listed below all offer scuba diving. Some may, however, combine a dive cruise with other activities such as fishing. Many of the smaller vessels are only available for private charters.

Most vessels operate out of Male', though with advance planning it's possible to fly to a distant tourist atoll and meet the boat there, saving many hours or even days of cruising time. Generally you must pay in advance with a bank transfer or credit card, while onboard expenses are settled in cash, unless prior arrangements are made.

The quality of the vessel, the service and amenities are often linked to the price of a cruise. The majority of vessels lack air conditioning, relying instead on natural airflow through the cabins. Meals are often served outside, though most boats have dining rooms for rainy days.

Few boats offer underwater camera rentals, but you may be able to rent one from your resort. Rental scuba gear is limited, so it's best to contact the associated resort in advance to reserve all the necessary items. If you plan to take certification or training courses, you'll also need to arrange those in advance.

Adventurer-1
Diving Adventure Maldives
M. Kurigum, Ithaa Goalhi, Male'
☎/fax: 326734 ☎ 783365
divemald@dhivehinet.net.mv
www.maldivesdiving.com
Length: 22m (72ft)
Number of cabins: 6
Max passenger capacity: 12

Atoll Explorer
Universal Enterprises
39 Orchid Magu, Male'
☎ 323080 fax: 322678
atexplorer@unisurf.com
www.unisurf.com
Length: 48m (157ft)

Number of cabins: 20
Max passenger capacity: 40

Baraabaru
Sea Explorers Associates
Violet Magu, Male'
☎ 316172 fax: 316783
seaexplo@dhivehinet.net.mv
Length: 18m (59ft)
Number of cabins: 4
Max passenger capacity: 10

Barutheela
Sporgasse 13
8010 Graz, Austria
☎ +43 316 81 25 48
fax: +43 316 81 25 89
info@baru-maldives.com

www.barutheela.com
Length: 30m (98ft)
Number of cabins: 6
Max passenger capacity: 18

Blue Dolphin
Corey Dolphin Travel, Male'
☎ 315439 fax: 321549
Length: 25m (82ft)
Number of cabins: 6
Max passenger capacity: 12

Blue Shark
M. Stella, Male'
☎ 327826/772069 fax: 326382
Length: 27m (89ft)
Number of cabins: 9
Max passenger capacity: 30

Safari Dive Boats (continued)

Cat Fish
AAA Travel & Tours
03-02 STO Trade Centre
Orchid Magu, Male'
☎ 316131 fax: 331726
trvlntrs@aaa.com.mv
www.aaa-resortsmaldives.com
Length: 15.3m (50ft)
Number of cabins: 5
Max passenger capacity: 10

Constanza
MV Kethi
Luxwood 3, Marine Drive, Male'
☎/fax: 312037
kethi@dhivehinet.net.mv
Length: 14m (46ft)
Number of cabins: 4
Max passenger capacity: 9

Cutty Shark
Great Land, Male'
☎ 327667/772576 fax: 327496
Length: 18m (59ft)
Number of cabins: 5
Max passenger capacity: 12

"Cyrus" the Love Boat
Atoll Vacations
H. Hithigasdhoshuge, Male'
☎ 315450/451
fax: 314783/323144
atvac@dhivehinet.net.mv
Length: 13.5m (44ft)
Number of cabins: 2
Max passenger capacity: 5

Dhandahelu II
Phoenix Hotels & Resorts
H. Fasmeeru
Ameer Ahmed Magu, Male'
☎ 323181 fax: 325499
phoenix@dhivehinet.net.mv
Length: 19m (62ft)
Number of cabins: 6
Max passenger capacity: 12

Dhinasha
Canopus Maldives
G. Maavehi, Buruzu Magu, Male'
☎ 321079 fax: 325397
mwahid@dhivehinet.net.mv
www.canopusmaldives.com
Length: 28m (92ft)
Number of cabins: 8
Max passenger capacity: 15

Discovery
Cyprea
25 Marine Drive, Male'
☎ 322451 fax: 323523
cyprea@dhivehinet.net.mv
Length: 20m (66ft)
Number of cabins: 3
Max passenger capacity: 12

Discovery 1
Marine Fauna Safari & Travel
2nd Floor, M. Kurimaa
Sabudheli Magu, Male'
☎ 771383 fax: 316153
info@maldivecruise.com
www.maldivecruise.com
Length: 32.5m (107ft)
Number of cabins: 11
Max passenger capacity: 25

Dolphin
Sea Explorers Associates
Violet Magu, Male'
☎ 316172 fax: 316783
seaexplo@dhivehinet.net.mv
www.seafariadventures.com
Length: 17m (56ft)
Number of cabins: 4
Max passenger capacity: 8

Eagle Ray
H. Fathihuge Ali, Male'
☎ 772659/771837 fax: 310782
Length: 30m (98ft)
Number of cabins: 7
Max passenger capacity: 14

Faiymini
Capital Travel & Tours
M. Feylige, 2nd Floor
Mihiri Magu, Male'
☎ 315089 fax: 320336
capital@dhivehinet.net.mv
www.faiymini.com
Length: 20m (66ft)
Number of cabins: 5
Max passenger capacity: 14

Fathuhul Bari
Sun Travels & Tours
H. Maley-thila
Meheli Goalhi, Male'
☎ 325977 fax: 320419
suntrvl@dhivehinet.net.mv
www.sunholidays.com
Length: 29m (95ft)
Number of cabins: 8
Max passenger capacity: 16

Fieyra
Paradise Holidays
1st Floor, Star Building, Male'
☎ 312090 fax: 312087
parahol@dhivehinet.net.mv
www.parahol.com
Length: 17m (56ft)
Number of cabins: 6
Max passenger capacity: 16

Finolhu
M. Kurimaa
Sabudheli Magu, Male'
☎ 318897/771325 fax: 321588
Length: 16m (53ft)
Number of cabins: 5
Max passenger capacity: 10

Flying Fish
Panorama Maldives
M. Muli, Sabudheli Magu, Male'
☎ 327066/67 or 337066
fax: 326542
panorama@dhivehinet.net.mv
www.panorama-maldives.com
Length: 26m (85ft)
Number of cabins: 7
Max passenger capacity: 14

Gahaa
Voyages Maldives
Narugis
Chandanee Magu, Male'
☎ 323617 fax: 325336
info@voyages.com.mv
www.voyagesmaldives.com
Length: 18.2m (60ft)
Number of cabins: 6
Max passenger capacity: 12

Get Wet
Secura, Male'
☎ 318919/771213 fax: 318817
Length: 30m (98ft)
Number of cabins: 8
Max passenger capacity: 45

Giritee
Alysen Services, Male'
☎ 321997 fax: 325601
alysen@dhivehinet.net.mv
Length: 23m (75ft)
Number of cabins: 6
Max passenger capacity: 16

Safari Dive Boats (continued)

Gomafulhu
Crown Tours Maldives
H. Sea Coast
30 Marine Drive, Male'
☎ 322432 fax: 312832
info@crowntoursmaldives.com
www.crowntoursmaldives.com
Length: 23m (75ft)
Number of cabins: 6
Max passenger capacity: 12

Gulfaam
Voyages Maldives
Narugis
Chandanee Magu, Male'
☎ 323617 fax: 325336
info@voyages.com.mv
www.voyagesmaldives.com
Length: 19.3m (63ft)
Number of cabins: 7
Max passenger capacity: 14

Hammer Head
Hammer Head Travel Agency
Male'
☎ 314837/771176
fax: 318354
Length: 28m (92ft)
Number of cabins: 5
Max passenger capacity: 12

Hammer Head II
Hammer Head Travel Agency
Male'
☎ 314837/771176 fax: 318354
Length: 34m (112ft)
Number of cabins: 7
Max passenger capacity: 16

Haveyli
Panorama Maldives
M. Muli, Sabudheli Magu, Male'
☎ 327066/67 or 337066
fax: 326542
panorama@dhivehinet.net.mv
www.panorama-maldives.com
Length: 30m (98ft)
Number of cabins: 11
Max passenger capacity: 20

Horizon
Blue Horizon
M. Mudhdhoo
Feeroaz Magu, Male'
☎ 321169 fax: 328797
bluehrzn@dhivehinet.net.mv
www.blue-horizon.com.mv
Length: 20m (66ft)

Number of cabins: 5
Max passenger capacity: 14

Isis Cruiser
Asdu Sun Island
H. Maamuli, Male'
☎ 445051/776310 fax: 440176
info@isiscruiser.com
www.isiscruiser.com
Length: 8m (26ft)
Number of cabins: 8
Max passenger capacity: 30

Jaariya
Interlink Maldives
H. Ashan Lodge
Vaijehay Magu, Male'
☎ 313537 fax: 313538
intlink@dhivehinet.net.mv
Length: 32m (105ft)
Number of cabins: 11
Max passenger capacity: 22

Jaquimac
MV Kethi
Luxwood 3, Marine Drive, Male'
☎/fax: 312037
kethi@dhivehinet.net.mv
Length: 14m (46ft)
Number of cabins: 3
Max passenger capacity: 8

Kaaviya
Phoenix Hotels & Resorts
H. Fasmeeru
Ameer Ahmed Magu, Male'
☎ 323181 fax: 325499
phoenix@dhivehinet.net.mv
Length: 20m (66ft)
Number of cabins: 6
Max passenger capacity: 12

Kamana
Crown Tours Maldives
H. Sea Coast
30 Marine Drive, Male'
☎ 322432 fax: 312832
info@crowntoursmaldives.com
www.crowntoursmaldives.com
Length: 28m (92ft)
Number of cabins: 7
Max passenger capacity: 14

Keema
Interlink Maldives
H. Ashan Lodge
Vaijehay Magu, Male'
☎ 313537 fax: 313538

intlink@dhivehinet.net.mv
Length: 27m (89ft)
Number of cabins: 6
Max passenger capacity: 12

Kethi
Voyages Maldives
Narugis
Chandanee Magu, Male'
☎ 323617 fax: 325336
info@voyages.com.mv
www.voyagesmaldives.com
Length: 19.5m (64ft)
Number of cabins: 7
Max passenger capacity: 14

Koimala
Voyages Maldives
Narugis
Chandanee Magu, Male'
☎ 323617 fax: 325336
info@voyages.com.mv
www.voyagesmaldives.com
Length: 23m (75ft)
Number of cabins: 7
Max passenger capacity: 14

Kudhi Boli
Phoenix Hotels & Resorts
H. Fasmeeru
Ameer Ahmed Magu, Male'
☎ 323181 fax: 325499
phoenix@dhivehinet.net.mv
Length: 19m (62ft)
Number of cabins: 5
Max passenger capacity: 10

Kureli
Phoenix Hotels & Resorts
H. Fasmeeru
Ameer Ahmed Magu, Male'
☎ 323181 fax: 325499
phoenix@dhivehinet.net.mv
Length: 21m (69ft)
Number of cabins: 6
Max passenger capacity: 12

Maarana
Interlink Maldives
H. Ashan Lodge
Vaijehay Magu, Male'
☎ 313537 fax: 313538
intlink@dhivehinet.net.mv
Length: 28m (92ft)
Number of cabins: 8
Max passenger capacity: 16

Safari Dive Boats (continued)

Maavahi
Travel Land Maldives
H. Cozy House
Samundhu Goalhi, Male'
☎ 316620 fax: 321058
info@tlmaldives.com
www.tlmaldives.com
Length: 26m (85ft)
Number of cabins: 8
Max passenger capacity: 16

Madivaru 7
Seafari Adventures
Via F. Frisi 20
20052 Monza, Italy
☎ +39 039 32 93 38
fax: +39 039 32 89 46
seafari_maldives@iol.it
www.seafariadventures.com
Length: 30m (100ft)
Number of cabins: 8
Max passenger capacity: 16

Madivaru 3
Seafari Adventures
Via F. Frisi 20
20052 Monza, Italy
☎ +39 039 32 93 38
fax: +39 039 32 89 46
seafari_maldives@iol.it
www.seafariadventures.com
Length: 24m (79ft)
Number of cabins: 6
Max passenger capacity: 11

Mandhoo
Phoenix Hotels & Resorts
H. Fasmeeru
Ameer Ahmed Magu, Male'
☎ 323181 fax: 325499
phoenix@dhivehinet.net.mv
Length: 21m (69ft)
Number of cabins: 6
Max passenger capacity: 12

Manthiri
Sea N See
2nd Floor, Oakum Building
Hadheebee Magu, Male'
☎ 325634 or 320323/4
fax: 325633
seansee@dhivehinet.net.mv
www.manthiri.com
Length: 26m (85ft)
Number of cabins: 6
Max passenger capacity: 12

Mas Hibaru
Mabaz Trade & Travels
M. Fehivinage, Male'
☎ 323335 fax: 328972
Length: 18m (59ft)
Number of cabins: 6
Max passenger capacity: 12

Moodhumaa
Muni Travels
M. Karadhuburi-aage
Shaheed Ali Higun, Male'
☎ 331512 fax: 331513
munitrav@dhivehinet.net.mv
www.munitravels.com
Length: 28m (92ft)
Number of cabins: 8
Max passenger capacity: 16

Moonimaa
Muni Travels
M. Karadhuburi-aage
Shaheed Ali Higun, Male'
☎ 331512 fax: 331513
munitrav@dhivehinet.net.mv
www.munitravels.com
Length: 26m (85ft)
Number of cabins: 6
Max passenger capacity: 12

Nasru Ali
Lif-Sham Travel & Tours
MTCC Building
Marine Drive, Male'
☎ 325386 fax: 320381
lift23@dhivehinet.net.mv
www.lifsham-holidays.com
Length: 25m (82ft)
Number of cabins: 6
Max passenger capacity: 14

Nasrumano
New Flower, K. Villingili 55
☎ 390097/390081 fax: 390098
Length: 25m (82ft)
Number of cabins: 4
Max passenger capacity: 8

Nautilus One
Nautico Maldives
H. Oleander, Male'
☎ 315253 fax: 324496
nautico@dhivehinet.net.mv
www.nautilus.at
Length: 31m (102ft)
Number of cabins: 8
Max passenger capacity: 16

Niru
Blue Horizon
M. Mudhdhoo
Feeroaz Magu, Male'
☎ 321169 fax: 328797
bluehrzn@dhivehinet.net.mv
www.blue-horizon.com.mv
Length: 16m (53ft)
Number of cabins: 3
Max passenger capacity: 8

Northrope
MV Kethi
Luxwood 3, Marine Drive
☎/fax: 312037
kethi@dhivehinet.net.mv
Length: 12m (39ft)
Number of cabins: 3
Max passenger capacity: 6

Ocean Safari
Travelin Maldives
STO Aifaanu Building, Male'
☎ 317717 fax: 314977
travelin@dhivehinet.net.mv
Length: 26m (85ft)
Number of cabins: 10
Max passenger capacity: 20

Orca
Panorama Maldives
M. Muli, Sabudheli Magu, Male'
☎ 327066/67 or 337066
fax: 326542
panorama@dhivehinet.net.mv
www.panorama-maldives.com
Length: 24m (79ft)
Number of cabins: 6
Max passenger capacity: 12

Panorama
Panorama Maldives
M. Muli, Sabudheli Magu, Male'
☎ 327066/67 or 337066
fax: 326542
panorama@dhivehinet.net.mv
www.panorama-maldives.com
Length: 17m (56ft)
Number of cabins: 4
Max passenger capacity: 8

Safari Dive Boats (continued)

Pretty Tombilli
H. Amsaa Villa, Male'
☎ 772051 ☎/fax: 333759
creative@dhivehinet.net.mv
tombilli@aol.com
www.tombilli.com
Length: 24m (79ft)
Number of cabins: 6
Max passenger capacity: 12

Rani
Eslire Maldives
Alikelegefaanu Magu, Male'
☎ 327438 fax: 313604
eslire@dhivehinet.net.mv
Length: 24m (79ft)
Number of cabins: 6
Max passenger capacity: 12

Rani 1
Eslire Maldives
Alikelegefaanu Magu, Male'
☎ 327438 fax: 313604
eslire@dhivehinet.net.mv
Length: 21m (69ft)
Number of cabins: 6
Max passenger capacity: 10

Sarah-1
Crown Tours Maldives
H. Sea Coast
30 Marine Drive, Male'
☎ 322432 fax: 312832
info@crowntoursmaldives.com
www.crowntoursmaldives.com
Length: 24m (79ft)
Number of cabins: 6
Max passenger capacity: 12

Sea Coral
Voyages Maldives
Narugis
Chandanee Magu, Male'
☎ 323617 fax: 325336
info@voyages.com.mv
www.voyagesmaldives.com
Length: 18.2m (60ft)

Number of cabins: 5
Max passenger capacity: 10

Sea Farer
Voyages Maldives
Narugis
Chandanee Magu, Male'
☎ 323617 fax: 325336
info@voyages.com.mv
www.voyagesmaldives.com
Length: 17m (56ft)
Number of cabins: 4
Max passenger capacity: 8

Sea Queen
Maldives Scuba Tours
Finningham Barns, Walsham Rd
Suffolk, IP14 4JG
United Kingdom
☎ +44 1449 780220
fax: +44 1449 780221
info@scubascuba.com
www.scubascuba.com
Length: 24m (79ft)
Number of cabins: 6
Max passenger capacity: 12

Shadas
Shadas
G. Nooraanee Fehi, Male'
☎ 774107 fax: 310179
shadas@shadas.com
www.shadas.com
Length: 16m (53ft)
Number of cabins: 4
Max passenger capacity: 7

Silvester
Yacht Tours Maldives, Male'
☎ 323028 fax: 310206
yachtour@dhivehinet.net.mv
Length: 30m (98ft)
Number of cabins: 8
Max passenger capacity: 16

Spirit
MV Kethi

Luxwood 3
Marine Drive, Male'
☎/fax: 312037
kethi@dhivehinet.net.mv
Length: 11m (36ft)
Number of cabins: 3
Max passenger capacity: 8

Sultana
MV Kethi
Luxwood 3
Marine Drive, Male'
☎/fax: 312037
kethi@dhivehinet.net.mv
Length: 11m (36ft)
Number of cabins: 3
Max passenger capacity: 6

Suwasa II
Phoenix Hotels & Resorts
H. Fasmeeru
Ameer Ahmed Magu, Male'
☎ 323181 fax: 325499
phoenix@dhivehinet.net.mv
Length: 16m (53ft)
Number of cabins: 4
Max passenger capacity: 11

Ummeedhu-5
Lif-Sham Travel & Tours
MTCC Building
01-04 Marine Drive, Male'
☎ 325386 fax: 320381
lift23@dhivehinet.net.mv
www.lifsham-holidays.com
Length: 23.5m (77ft)
Number of cabins: 6
Max passenger capacity: 18

Warrior
4 Aaburuzu Higun, Male'
☎ 316146 fax: 314471
noomara@dhivehinet.net.mv
Length: 15m (49ft)
Number of cabins: 4
Max passenger capacity: 8

Accommodations

Accommodation options in the Maldives consist of the outlying resort islands and relatively simple but clean guesthouses and hotels in Male'. Many of the resorts are managed by and cater to people of specific nationalities (Italian, German, etc.). The staff typically speaks at least some English, but if you're not well versed in the primary language spoken at a resort, you may want to look elsewhere for accommodations.

Transfer to the resort islands is by dhoni, speedboat or seaplane. To reach Male', take a dhoni directly from the airport. Most hotels there are within walking distance of the dhoni dock, though if you have heavy luggage, you may opt for a short taxi ride. Some hotels and resorts will prearrange your transport from the airport. See Practicalities, page 24, for more information.

All resort islands feature an on-site dive center, each offering a variety of services. Available courses range from basic certification to specialty instruction. Dive gear is widely available for rent, and some shops sell equipment. Many dive centers have separate email addresses and websites, while others are reachable through their associated resort.

Male'

Athamaa Palace Hotel
G. Dhivehi Atha, Majeedi Magu
☎ 313118 fax: 328828

Beevaa Inn
M. Thilafahige
Shaheed Ali Higun
☎ 316416 fax: 318297

Blue Diamond Guesthouse
Ma. Bright Blue
Badifasgandu Magu
☎ 326125 fax: 316404
bdiamond@dhivehinet.net.mv

Buruneege Residence
H. Buruneege
Hithaffinivaa Magu
☎ 330011 fax: 330022

Central Hotel
G. Sanoaraage
Rahdhebai Magu
☎ 317766 fax: 315383
central@dhivehinet.net.mv

City Motel
H. Caribbean, Kaasinjee Magu
☎ 310004 fax: 310005

City Palace
H. Hiriyadhoo, Filigas Higun
☎ 312152 fax: 322154
citymale@dhivehinet.net.mv

Classic Inn
M. Zameen, Iramaa Magu
☎ 324311 fax: 317257

Holiday Lodge
H. Fujeyra, Marine Drive
☎ 310279 fax: 326542

Ikaz Hotel
M. Angaagiri
Shaheed Ali Higun
☎ 332891 fax: 332895

Kai Lodge
H. Mandhuedhuruge
Violet Magu
☎ 328742 fax: 328738

Kam Hotel
H. Roanuge, Meheli Goalhi
☎ 320611 fax: 320614
kamhotel@dhivehinet.net.mv

Maadhuni Inn
H. Maadhuni
Ameer Ahmed Magu
☎ 322824 fax: 322597
maadhuni@dhivehinet.net.mv

Maafaru Guesthouse
M. Maafaru, Champa Magu
☎ 313558 fax: 318632

Maagiri Lodge
H. Maagiri, Marine Drive
☎ 322576 fax: 328787

Male' Tour Inn
H. Ranthudu, Shaheed Ali Higun
☎ 326220 fax: 325213

Marble Tourist Lodge
M. Marble
Knaba'aisa Rani Higun
☎ 326237 fax: 310972

Nasandhura Palace Hotel
Marine Drive
☎ 323380 fax: 320822
nasndhra@dhivehinet.net.mv

Relax Inn
H. Olive, Ameer Ahmed Magu
☎ 314531/2 fax: 314533
relaxinn@dhivehinet.net.mv
www.hotelrelaxinn.com

Royal Inn
M. Honey Dew
Izzudhdheen Magu
☎ 320573 fax: 320108

Sea Lodge
M. Viludholhi, Marine Drive
☎ 330066 fax: 330022

Transit Inn
Ma. Dheyliaage
Maaveyo Magu
☎ 320420 fax: 329665

Villingili View Inn
M. Raaverige, Majeedi Magu
☎ 321135/318696 fax: 325213

North & South Male' Atolls (Kaafu)

Angsana Resort & Spa
Dhirham Travels & Chandling
5th Floor, Filaa Building
Koli Umar Maniku Goalhi, Male'
☎ 443502/323369
fax: 445933/324752
reservations@angsana.com
www.angsana.com
Distance to airport: 17km
(11 miles)
Number of rooms: 49

Asdu Sun Island
H. Maamuli, Male'
☎ 445051/322149
fax: 445051/324300
info@asdu.com
www.asdu.com
Dive center:
info@submaldive.com
www.submaldive.com
Distance to airport: 32km
(20 miles)
Number of rooms: 30

Bandos Island Resort
Deens Villa, Filigas Magu, Male'
☎ 440088/325529
fax: 443877/321026
info@bandos.com.mv
www.bandos.com
Dive center:
dive@bandos.com.mv
Distance to airport: 8km
(5 miles)
Number of rooms: 225

Banyan Tree Vabbinfaru
Dhirham Travels & Chandling
5th Floor, Filaa Building
Koli Umar Maniku Goalhi, Male'
☎ 443147/323369
fax: 443843/324752
maldives@banyantree.com
www.banyantree.com
Distance to airport: 16km
(10 miles)
Number of rooms: 48

Baros Holiday Resort
Universal Enterprises
39 Orchid Magu, Male'
☎ 440017/323080
fax: 443497/322678
baros@unisurf.com
www.unisurf.com

Dive center:
divebaros@hotmail.com
www.baros-diving.com
Distance to airport: 14km
(9 miles)
Number of rooms: 77

Biyadhoo Island Resort
H. Maarandhooge
Meheli Goalhi, Male'
☎ 447171/324699
fax: 447272/327014
resvn@biyadoo.com.mv
Dive center:
jsdw@biyadoo.com.mv
www.divingworld-maldives.com
Distance to airport: 29km
(18 miles)
Number of rooms: 96

Boduhithi Coral Island
Holiday Club Maldives
2nd Floor
H. Gadhamoo Building, Male'
☎ 445905/313938
fax: 442634/313939
boduhithi@clubvacanze.com.mv
www.clubvacanze.com
Distance to airport: 29km
(18 miles)
Number of rooms: 87

Bolifushi Island Resort
Gateway Maldives
4th Floor, Alia Building, Male'
☎ 443517/317527
fax: 445924/317529
admin@bolifushi.com
www.bolifushi.com
Distance to airport: 12km
(7 miles)
Number of rooms: 55

Club Med Faru
Majeedi Bazaar
1 Ibrahim Hassan Didi Magu
Male'
☎ 442017 fax: 442415
gesfar@clubmed-faru.com.mv
www.clubmed.com
Dive center:
info@euro-divers.com
www.euro-divers.com
Distance to airport: 2km
(1 mile)
Number of rooms: 152

Club Rannalhi
Jetan Travel Services
7th Floor
STO Aifaanu Building, Male'
☎ 442688/323323
fax: 442035/317993
reserve@rannalhi.com.mv
Distance to airport: 34km
(21 miles)
Number of rooms: 116

Cocoa Beach
392 Izzudhdheen Magu, Male'
☎ 441818/325529
fax: 441919/318992
info@cocoamaldives.com.mv
www.cocoamaldives.com
Dive center:
opm@dhivehinet.net.mv
www.oceanparadise.com.mv
Distance to airport: 30km
(19 miles)
Number of rooms: 30

Dhigufinolhu Island Resort
H. Athireege Aage
Lotus Goalhi, Male'
☎ 443599/314008
fax: 443886/327058
dhigu@dhigufinolhu.com
www.dhigufinolhu.com
Dive center:
scubasub@palmtree.com.mv
Distance to airport: 21km
(13 miles)
Number of rooms: 100

Embudu Village
Kaimoo Travels & Hotel Services
H. Roanuge, Male'
☎ 444776/322212
fax: 442673/318057
embvil@dhivehinet.net.mv
www.embuduvillage.com.mv
Dive center:
diverlan@dhivehinet.net.mv
www.diverland.com
Distance to airport: 8km
(5 miles)
Number of rooms: 118

North & South Male' Atolls (Kaafu) (continued)

Eriyadu Island Resort
AAA Hotels & Resorts
3rd Floor
03-02 STO Trade Centre
Orchid Magu, Male'
☎ 444487/316131
fax: 445926/331726
eriyadu@aaa.com.mv
www.aaa-resortsmaldives.com
Dive center:
wernerlau@aol.com
www.wernerlau.com
Distance to airport: 42km
(26 miles)
Number of rooms: 57

Fihalhohi Tourist Resort
Dhirham Travels & Chandling
5th Floor, Filaa Building
Koli Umar Maniku Goalhi, Male'
☎ 442903/323369
fax: 443803/324752
fiha@dhivehinet.net.mv
www.fihalhohi.net
Distance to airport: 28km
(17 miles)
Number of rooms: 128

**Four Seasons Resort
Maldives at Kuda Huraa**
☎ 444888 fax: 441188
info@kudahuraa.com
www.fourseasons.com/maldives
Dive center:
fsrmdive@dhivehinet.net.mv
Distance to airport: 20km
(12 miles)
Number of rooms: 106

Full Moon Beach Resort
Universal Enterprises
39 Orchid Magu, Male'
☎ 442010/323080
fax: 441979/322678
fullmoon@unisurf.com
www.unisurf.com
Dive center:
info@euro-divers.com
www.euro-divers.com
Distance to airport: 6km
(4 miles)
Number of rooms: 156

Fun Island
Villa Hotels
Villa Building
Ibrahim Hassan Didi Magu
Male'

☎ 444558/316161
fax: 443958/314565
info@fun-island.com.mv
www.villahotels.com
Dive center:
ddcfun@delphis.com.mv
www.delphisdiving.com
Distance to airport: 38km
(24 miles)
Number of rooms: 100

Gasfinolhu Island Resort
Imad's Agency
Chandanee Magu, Male'
☎ 442078/323441
fax: 445941/322964
Distance to airport: 23km
(14 miles)
Number of rooms: 40

Giravaru Tourist Resort
TBI Maldives
Safari Buildings, Male'
☎ 440440/318422
fax: 444818/318505
giravaru@dhivehinet.net.mv
www.giravaru.com
Dive center:
dive@blueplanet.com.mv
Distance to airport: 11km
(7 miles)
Number of rooms: 65

Helengeli Tourist Village
H. Karanka Villa
Marine Drive, Male'
☎ 444615/328544
fax: 442881/325150
engeli88@dhivehinet.net.mv
www.helengeli-maldives.com
Dive center:
helidive1@herbie.com.mv
www.oceanpro-diveteam.com
Distance to airport: 43km
(27 miles)
Number of rooms: 50

Hudhuveli Beach Resort
H. Jazeera, Marine Drive, Male'
☎ 443982/325529
fax: 443849/321026
hudhuveli@flashmail.com
Distance to airport: 12km
(7 miles)
Number of rooms: 44

Kandooma Tourist Resort
H. Javaafa
Finihiya Goalhi, Male'
☎ 444452/323360
fax: 445948/326880
info@kandooma.com
www.kandooma.com
Dive center:
aquanaut@dhivehinet.net.mv
www.aquanaut-tauchreisen.de
Distance to airport: 35km
(22 miles)
Number of rooms: 124

Kanifinolhu Resort
Cyprea
25 Marine Drive, Male'
☎ 443152/322451
fax: 444859/323523
kanifin@dhivehinet.net.mv
www.kanifinolhu.com
Dive center:
info@euro-divers.com
www.euro-divers.com
Distance to airport: 19km
(12 miles)
Number of rooms: 150

**Kurumba Village
Tourist Resort**
Universal Enterprises
39 Orchid Magu, Male'
☎ 442324/323080
fax: 443885/322678
kurumba@unisurf.com
www.unisurf.com
Dive center:
info@euro-divers.com
www.euro-divers.com
Distance to airport: 3km
(2 miles)
Number of rooms: 180

Laguna Beach Resort
Universal Enterprises
39 Orchid Magu, Male'
☎ 445906/323080
fax: 443041/322678
laguna@unisurf.com
www.unisurf.com
Distance to airport: 12km
(7 miles)
Number of rooms: 132

North & South Male' Atolls (Kaafu) (continued)

Lohifushi Island Resort
Altaf Enterprises
3 Koli Umar Maniku Goalhi
Male'
☎ 443451/323378
fax: 441908/324783
lohifush@dhivehinet.net.mv
www.lohifushi.com
Distance to airport: 19km
(12 miles)
Number of rooms: 127

Makunudu Island
Sunland Hotels
04-01 STO Trade Centre, Male'
☎ 446464/324658
fax: 446565/325543
makunudu@dhivehinet.net.mv
www.makunudu.com
Distance to airport: 38km
(24 miles)
Number of rooms: 36

Meeru Island Resort
Champa Trade & Travels
Champa Building, Male'
☎ 443157/314149
fax: 445946/314150
info@meeru.com
www.meeru.com
Dive center:
oceanpro@dhivehinet.net.mv
www.oceanpro-diveteam.com
Distance to airport: 37km
(23 miles)
Number of rooms: 227

Nakatchafushi Tourist Resort
Universal Enterprises
39 Orchid Magu, Male'
☎ 443847/323080
fax: 442665/322678
nakatcha@unisurf.com
www.unisurf.com
Distance to airport: 24km
(15 miles)
Number of rooms: 51

Paradise Island
Villa Hotels
Villa Building
Ibrahim Hassan Didi Magu
Male'
☎ 440011/316161
fax: 440022/314565

info@paradise-island.com.mv
www.villahotels.com
Dive center:
ddcpar@delphis.com.mv
www.delphisdiving.com
Distance to airport: 10km
(6 miles)
Number of rooms: 260

Reethi Rah Resort
Ma. Sheerazeege
Sheeraazee Goalhi, Male'
☎ 441905/323758
fax: 441906/328842
rrresort@dhivehinet.net.mv
Dive center:
info@euro-divers.com
www.euro-divers.com
Distance to airport: 35km
(22 miles)
Number of rooms: 60

Rihiveli Beach Resort
Jamalee Store, Shop 4
Ahmadhee Bazaar, Male'
☎ 441994/322421
fax: 440052/320976
info@rihiveli-island.com
www.rihiveli-island.com
Dive center:
rihiveli@euro-divers.com
www.euro-divers.com
Distance to airport: 40km
(25 miles)
Number of rooms: 48

Summer Island Village
H. Roanuge, Male'
☎ 443088/322212
fax: 441910/318057
siv@dhivehinet.net.mv
www.summerislandvillage.com
Dive center:
michael_lydia@web.de
www.dive-summer-island-
village.de
Distance to airport: 35km
(22 miles)
Number of rooms: 108

Taj Coral Reef Resort
Taj Maldives
10 Medhuziyaarai Magu, Male'
☎ 441948/317530
fax: 443884/314059

tajcr@dhivehinet.net.mv
www.tajhotels.com
Dive center:
bluein@dhivehinet.net.mv
www.blueinmaldives.com
Distance to airport: 32km
(20 miles)
Number of rooms: 65

Taj Exotica Maldives
Taj Maldives
10 Medhuziyaarai Magu, Male'
☎ 444451/317530
fax: 445925/314059
tajlr@dhivehinet.net.mv
www.tajhotels.com
Distance to airport: 9km
(6 miles)
Number of rooms: 64

Tari Sporting Village
Treasure Island
2 Ahmadhee Bazaar, Male'
☎ 440013/316454
fax: 440012/310206
tari@tarivillage.com.mv
www.tarivillage.com
Distance to airport: 13km
(8 miles)
Number of rooms: 24

Thulhagiri Island Resort
H. Jazeera, Marine Drive, Male'
☎ 445930/322844
fax: 445939/321026
reserve@thulhaagiri.com.mv
Dive center:
infothulha@tgidiving.com
www.tgidiving.com
Distance to airport: 13km
(8 miles)
Number of rooms: 58

Vadoo Island Resort
H. Maarandhooge
Irumatheebai, Filigas Magu
Male'
☎ 443976/325844
fax: 443397/325846
vadoo@vadoo.com.mv
Dive center:
diving@vadoo.com.mv
Distance to airport: 8km
(5 miles)
Number of rooms: 31

North & South Male' Atolls (Kaafu) (continued)

Veligandu Huraa
Palm Tree Island
H. Athireege Aage
Lotus Goalhi, Male'
☎ 443882/314008
fax: 440009/327058
veli@veliganduhuraa.com
www.veliganduhuraa.com

Dive center:
scubasub@palmtree.com.mv
Distance to airport: 19km
(12 miles)
Number of rooms: 23

Villivaru Island Resort
H. Maarandhooge
Meheli Goalhi, Male'

☎ 447070/324699
fax: 447272/327014
resvn@biyadoo.com.mv
Dive center:
jsdw@biyadoo.com.mv
www.divingworld-maldives.com
Distance to airport: 29km
(18 miles)
Number of rooms: 60

Felidhoo Atoll (Vaavu)

Alimatha Aquatic Resort
Safari Tours
Chandanee Magu, Male'
☎ 450575/323524
fax: 450544/322516
alidivebase@hotmail.com

Distance to airport: 52km
(32 miles)
Number of rooms: 102

Dhiggiri Tourist Resort
Safari Tours
Chandanee Magu, Male'

☎ 450593/323524
fax: 450592/322516
mmtours@dhivehinet.net.mv
Distance to airport: 48km
(30 miles)
Number of rooms: 45

Mulaku Atoll (Meemu)

Hakuraa Club
FantaSea World Investments
H. Noouaraha
Roashanee Magu, Male'
☎ 460014/313738
fax: 460013/326264
hakuraa@dhivehinet.net.mv
www.johnkeellshotels.com
Dive center:
liveaboa@dhivehinet.net.mv

Distance to airport: 130km
(81 miles)
Number of rooms: 70

Medhufushi Island Resort
AAA Hotels & Resorts
3rd Floor
03-02 STO Trade Centre
Orchid Magu, Male'
☎ 460026/316131

fax: 460027/331726
medhu@aaa.com.mv
www.aaa-resortsmaldives.com
Dive center:
wernerlau@aol.com
www.wernerlau.com
Distance to airport: 129km
(80 miles)
Number of rooms: 120

Addu Atoll (Seenu)

Equator Village
Gan Invest
H. Maagala
Meheli Goalhi, Male'
☎ 588721/322212

fax: 588020/318057
equator@dhivehinet.net.mv
Dive center:
diverland@dhivehinet.net.mv
www.diverland.com

Distance to airport: 1km
(.6 mile)
Number of rooms: 78

South & North Nilandhoo Atolls (Dhaalu & Faafu)

Filitheyo Island Resort
AAA Hotels & Resorts
3rd Floor
03-02 STO Trade Centre
Orchid Magu, Male'
☎ 460025/316131
fax: 460024/331726
fili@aaa.com.mv
www.aaa-resortsmaldives.com
Dive center:

wernerlau@aol.com
www.wernerlau.com
Distance to airport: 121km
(75 miles)
Number of rooms: 125

Velavaru Island Resort
STO Trade Centre
Orchid Magu, Male'
☎ 460028/315287

fax: 460029/315286
info@velavaru.com.mv
www.velavaru.com
Dive center:
oceanpro@velavaru.com
www.oceanpro-diveteam.com
Distance to airport: 150km
(93 miles)
Number of rooms: 84

South & North Nilandhoo Atolls (Dhaalu & Faafu) (continued)

Vilu Reef Resort
Sun Travels & Tours
H. Maley-thila
Meheli Goalhi, Male'
☎ 460011/325977

fax: 460022/320419
info@vilureef.com.mv
www.vilureef.com
Dive center:
diveexplorer@wanadoo.fr

www.diveexplorer.com
Distance to airport: 129km
(80 miles)
Number of rooms: 68

Ari Atoll (Alifu)

Angaga Island Resort
MTCC Building
Marine Drive, Male'
☎ 450510/313523
fax: 450520/313522
angaga@dhivehinet.net.mv
Dive center:
tauchreisen@sub-aqua.de
www.sub-aqua.de
Distance from airport: 85km
(53 miles)
Number of rooms: 50

AriBeach Resort
1st Floor, 35 Marine Drive
Male'
☎ 450513/321930
fax: 450512/327355
aribeach@dhivehinet.net.mv
www.aribeach.com
Dive center:
aribeach@euro-divers.com
www.euro-divers.com
Distance to airport: 104km
(64 miles)
Number of rooms: 106

Athurugau Island Resort
M. Veeza
Dhambu Goalhi, Male'
☎ 450508/310489
fax: 450574/310390
athadmin@dhivehinet.net.mv
www.planhotel.ch
Dive center: athu@thecrab.com
www.thecrab.com
Distance to airport: 90km
(56 miles)
Number of rooms: 46

Bathala Island Resort
Bir Hotel Management Private
H. Kinolhas
Abadhahufaa Magu, Male'
☎ 450587/317993
fax: 450558/324628
bir0587@dhivehinet.net.mv

www.aitkenspence.com/bathala
Distance to airport: 56km
(35 miles)
Number of rooms: 38

**Dhidhdhoofinolhu
Watervillage**
1st Floor, 35 Marine Drive
Male'
☎ 450513/321930
fax: 450512/327355
info@watervillage.com
www.watervillage.com
Dive center:
aribeach@euro-divers.com
www.euro-divers.com
Distance to airport: 104km
(64 miles)
Number of rooms: 52

Ellaidhoo Tourist Resort
Travelin Maldives
STO Aifaanu Building, Male'
☎ 450514/317717
fax: 450586/314977
travelin@dhivehinet.net.mv
www.ellaidhoo.com
Dive center:
tauchreisen@sub-aqua.de
www.sub-aqua.de
Distance to airport: 36km
(22 miles)
Number of rooms: 50

Fesdu Fun Island
Universal Enterprises
39 Orchid Magu, Male'
☎ 450541/323080
fax: 450547/322678
fesdu@unisurf.com
www.unisurf.com
Distance to airport: 72km
(45 miles)
Number of rooms: 60

Gangehi Island Resort
Holiday Club Maldives
2nd Floor
H. Gadhamoo Building, Male'

☎ 450505/313938
fax: 450506/313939
gangehi@clubvacanze.com.mv
www.clubvacanze.com
Distance to airport: 77km
(48 miles)
Number of rooms: 25

Halaveli Holiday Village
Eastinvest
H. Akiri, Marine Drive, Male'
☎ 450559/322719
fax: 450564/323463
halaveli@dhivehinet.net.mv
www.halaveli.com
Distance to airport: 62km
(38 miles)
Number of rooms: 56

Holiday Island
Villa Hotels
Villa Building
Ibrahim Hassan Didi Magu
Male'
☎ 450011/316161
fax: 450022/314565
info@holiday-island.com.mv
www.villahotels.com
Dive center:
calypso@dhivehinet.net.mv
Distance to airport: 97km
(60 miles)
Number of rooms: 142

Kuda Rah Island Resort
Holiday Club Maldives
2nd Floor
H. Gadhamoo Building, Male'
☎ 450610/313938
fax: 450550/313939
kudarah@clubvacanze.com.mv
www.clubvacanze.com
Distance to airport: 89km
(55 miles)
Number of rooms: 30

Ari Atoll (Alifu) (continued)

Kuramathi Blue Lagoon
Universal Enterprises
39 Orchid Magu, Male'
☎ 450579/323080
fax: 450531/322678
kbluelagoon@unisurf.com
www.unisurf.com
Dive center:
info@rasdhoodivers.com
www.rasdhoodivers.com
Distance to airport: 70km
(43 miles)
Number of rooms: 50

Kuramathi Cottage Club
Universal Enterprises
39 Orchid Magu, Male'
☎ 450532/323080
fax: 450642/322678
kcottageclub@unisurf.com
www.unisurf.com
Dive center:
info@rasdhoodivers.com
www.rasdhoodivers.com
Distance to airport: 70km
(43 miles)
Number of rooms: 80

Kuramathi Village
Universal Enterprises
39 Orchid Magu, Male'
☎ 450622/323080
fax: 450556/322678
kvillage@unisurf.com
www.unisurf.com
Dive center:
info@rasdhoodivers.com
www.rasdhoodivers.com
Distance to airport: 70km
(43 miles)
Number of rooms: 151

Lily Beach Resort
Lily Hotels
1 Orchid Magu, Male'
☎ 450013/317464
fax: 450646/317466
info@lilybeach.com
www.lilybeach.com
Dive center:
oceanpro@dhivehinet.net.mv
www.oceanpro-diveteam.com
Distance to airport: 81km
(50 miles)
Number of rooms: 85

Maayafushi Island Resort
Star Resorts & Hotels
Opera Building
Chandanee Magu, Male'
☎ 450588/320097
fax: 450568/326658
maaya@dhivehinet.net.mv
Distance to airport: 63km
(39 miles)
Number of rooms: 60

Machchafushi Island Resort
H. Ocean View, 1st Floor
2 Marine Drive, Male'
☎ 454545/317080
fax: 454546/318014
info@machchafushi.com
www.machchafushi.com
Dive center:
tauchreisen@sub-aqua.de
www.sub-aqua.de
Distance to airport: 87km
(54 miles)
Number of rooms: 58

Madoogali Tourist Resort
H. Henveyruge
Medhuziyaarai Magu, Male'
☎ 450581/317975
fax: 450554/317974
madugali@dhivehinet.net.mv
Distance to airport: 72km
(45 miles)
Number of rooms: 50

**Maldives Hilton on
Rangali Island**
Crown Co., Marine Drive, Male'
☎ 450629/322432
fax: 450619/324009
info@maldiveshilton.com.mv
www.maldives.hilton.com
Dive center:
subranap@dhivehinet.net.mv
www.sub-aqua.de
Distance to airport: 97km
(60 miles)
Number of rooms: 150

Mirihi Island Resort
☎ 450500
fax: 450501
mirihi@dhivehinet.net.mv
www.mirihi.com
Dive center:
diving@mirihi.com.mv

www.sub-aqua.de
Distance to airport: 85km
(53 miles)
Number of rooms: 35

Moofushi Resort
Raiyvilla Higun, Male'
☎ 450517/326141
fax: 450509/313237
moofushi@dhivehinet.net.mv
www.moofushi.com
Distance to airport: 80km
(50 miles)
Number of rooms: 60

Nika Hotel
☎ 450516 fax: 450577
nika_htl@dhivehinet.net.mv
www.nikamaldive.com
Dive center: nika@nika.com.mv
www.nika.com.mv
Distance to airport: 74km
(46 miles)
Number of rooms: 27

Ranveli Village
Guardian Agency
M. Velidhooge
Dhambu Goalhi, Male'
☎ 450570/316921
fax: 450523/316922
ranveli@gardian.com.mv
www.ranveli-maldives.com
Distance to airport: 77km
(48 miles)
Number of rooms: 56

Sun Island
Villa Hotels
Villa Building
Ibrahim Hassan Didi Magu
Male'
☎ 450088/316161
fax: 450099/314565
info@sun-island.com.mv
www.villahotels.com
Dive center:
info@divingatthemaldives.com
www.divingatthemaldives.com
Distance to airport: 107km
(66 miles)
Number of rooms: 350

Ari Atoll (Alifu) (continued)

Thudufushi Island Resort
Voyages Maldives
Narugis, Chandanee Magu
Male'
☎ 450597/323617
fax: 450515/325336
admin@thudufushi.com.mv
www.planhotel.com
Dive center:
thudu@thecrab.com
www.thecrab.com
Distance to airport: 81km
(50 miles)
Number of rooms: 47

Twin Island
Universal Enterprises
39 Orchid Magu, Male'
☎ 450596/323080
fax: 450527/322678
twins@unisurf.com
www.unisurf.com
Distance to airport: 96km
(60 miles)
Number of rooms: 40

Vakarufalhi Island Resort
3rd Floor, Champa Building
Male'
☎ 450004/315287
fax: 450007/315286
info@vakaru.com
www.vakaru.com
Dive center:
vakarufalhi@prodivers.com
www.prodivers.com
Distance to airport: 90km
(56 miles)
Number of rooms: 50

Velidhu Island Resort
Travel Club
H. Noouaraha
Roashanee Magu, Male'
☎ 450551/313738
fax: 450630/326264
velidhu@dhivehinet.net.mv
www.johnkeellshotels.com
Dive center:
info@euro-divers.com
www.euro-divers.com
Distance to airport: 85km
(53 miles)
Number of rooms: 100

Veligandu Island Resort
Crown Tours Maldives
H. Sea Coast, 30 Marine Drive
Male'
☎ 450519/322432
fax: 450648/312832
info@veliganduisland.com
www.veliganduisland.com
Dive center:
oceanpro@dhivehinet.net.mv
www.oceanpro-diveteam.com
Distance to airport: 51km
(32 miles)
Number of rooms: 73

Vilamendhoo Island Resort
AAA Hotels & Resorts
3rd Floor, 03-02 STO Trade
Centre, Orchid Magu, Male'
☎ 450637/316131
fax: 450639/331726
vilamndu@aaa.com.mv
www.aaa-resortsmaldives.com
Dive center:
wernerlau@aol.com
www.wernerlau.com
Distance to airport: 82km
(51 miles)
Number of rooms: 141

South & North Maalhosmadulu Atolls (Baa & Raa)

Coco Palm Resort & Spa
Sunland Hotels
04-01 STO Trade Centre, Male'
☎ 230011/324658
fax: 230022/325543
cocopalm@sunland.com.mv
www.cocopalm.com.mv
Dive center:
oceanpro@dhivehinet.net.mv
www.oceanpro-diveteam.com
Distance to airport: 124km
(77 miles)
Number of rooms: 98

Khihaadhuffaru
Athama Marine
Lonuziyaarai Magu, Male'
☎ 230346/320157
fax: 230347/327748
athamar@dhivehinet.net.mv
Distance to airport: 105km
(65 miles)
Number of rooms: 100

Meedhupparu Island Resort
Cowrie Investment
STO Aifaanu Building
Marine Drive, Male'
☎ 237700/315236
fax: 235500/315237
admin@meedhupparu.com.mv
www.aitkenspencehotels.com
Dive center:
meedhu@thecrab.com
www.thecrab.com
Distance to airport: 130km
(81 miles)
Number of rooms: 215

Reethi Beach Resort
Magic Kingdom Resorts
1st Floor, 1-7 M. Velidhooge
Dhambu Goalhi, Male'
☎ 232626/316921
fax: 232727/316922
info@reethibeach.com.mv
www.reethibeach.com

Dive center:
dive@reethibeach.com.mv
www.sea-explorer.com
Distance to airport: 105km
(65 miles)
Number of rooms: 100

Royal Island
Villa Hotels
Villa Building
Ibrahim Hassan Didi Magu
Male'
☎ 230088/316161
fax: 230099/314565
info@royal-island.com.mv
www.villahotels.com
Dive center:
ddcroy@delphis.com.mv
www.delphisdiving.com
Distance to airport: 110km
(68 miles)
Number of rooms: 150

South & North Maalhosmadulu Atolls (Baa & Raa) (continued)

Soneva Fushi Resort & Spa
Bunny Holdings BVI
2nd Floor
4/3 Faamudheyri Magu, Male'
☎ 230304/326685

fax: 230374/324660
sonresa@soneva.com.mv
http://six-senses.com/
soneva-fushi
Dive center:
soleni@dhivehinet.net.mv

www.soleni.com
Distance to airport: 97km
(60 miles)
Number of rooms: 65

Faadhippolhu Atoll (Lhaviyani)

Kanuhura Sun Resort & Spa
Manaam Building
2/1 Neelafaru Magu, Male'
☎ 230044/313739
fax: 230033/331781
info@kanuhura.com
www.kanuhura.com
Dive center:
info@subventures.com
www.subventures.com
Distance to airport: 126km
(78 miles)
Number of rooms: 100

Komandoo Island Resort
4th Floor, Champa Building
Male'
☎ 231010/326545

fax: 231011/326544
info@komandoo.com
www.komandoo.com
Dive center:
komandoo@prodivers.com
www.prodivers.com
Distance to airport: 129km
(80 miles)
Number of rooms: 45

Kuredu Island Resort
Champa Trade & Travels
Champa Building, Male'
☎ 230337/326545
fax: 230332/326544
info@kuredu.com
www.kuredu.com

Dive center:
kuredu@prodivers.com
www.prodivers.com
Distance to airport: 129km
(80 miles)
Number of rooms: 300

Palm Beach Island
Sun Sporting Holidays
29 Marine Drive, Male'
☎ 230084/331997
fax: 230091/332001
info@palmbeachmaldives.com
www.palmbeachmaldives.com
Dive center: macamald@tin.it
Distance to airport: 129km
(80 miles)
Number of rooms: 100

Tourist Office

The Maldives Tourism Promotion Board offers a wealth of free information about the country in general as well as specific information about each of the atolls, up-to-date information on each of the resorts and most of the safari vessels, current weather, events and much more.

Maldives Tourism Promotion Board
4th Floor, Bank of Maldives Building
Marine Drive, Male'
☎ 323228 fax: 323229
mtpb@visitmaldives.com
www.visitmaldives.com

Index

dive sites covered in this book appear in **bold** type

Lonely Planet Pisces Books

The **Diving & Snorkeling** guides cover top destinations worldwide. Beautifully illustrated with full-color photos throughout, the series explores the best diving and snorkeling areas and prepares divers for what to expect when they get there. Each site is described in detail, with information on suggested ability levels, depth, visibility and, of course, marine life. There's basic topside information as well for each destination.

Also check out dive guides to:

Australia: Southeast Coast	Cocos Island	Pacific Northwest	Tahiti
Bahamas	Curaçao	Papua New Guinea	& French Polynesia
Baja California	Dominica	Puerto Rico	Texas
Belize	Guam & Yap	Scotland	Trinidad & Tobago
Bermuda	Jamaica	Seychelles	Turks & Caicos
Bonaire	Monterey Peninsula &	Southern California	Vanuatu
Chuuk Lagoon, Pohnpei & Kosrae	Northern California	& the Channel Islands	